K.G——

Harold and Joan

In loving memory of
Harold, Joan and Ann

Crumps Barn Studio
Crumps Barn, Syde, Cheltenham GL53 9PN
www.crumpsbarnstudio.co.uk

Cover design and title page illustration by Lorna Gray
All images copyright © Karen Geraldine Croft 2022

Printed in Gloucestershire on FSC certified paper by Severn,
a carbon neutral company

ISBN 978-1-915067-18-0

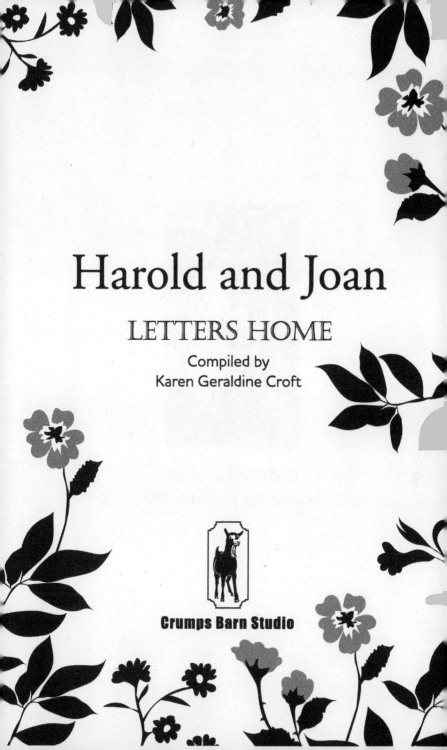

Harold and Joan

LETTERS HOME

Compiled by
Karen Geraldine Croft

Crumps Barn Studio

Harold and Joan on their wedding day, 11 August 1932

FOREWORD

When my mother and I were clearing out my grandmother's house over 20 years ago we came across a bundle of letters tied up with a narrow strip of blue ribbon. They were found in a drawer of a built-in dresser in the 'back room'. This drawer also contained various documents, medals, postcards and 'souvenirs' from my grandad's time in service during the Second World War. Allocated as 'keep', the war finds were carefully packed, removed and stored.

In 2019 I finally got round to sorting through possessions stored in the attic and rediscovered grandad's box of bits. I passed the bundle of letters to my mother to read in their original faded and fragile format before typing them up and putting them into some sort of chronological order. Not all the letters are complete, and my grandmother's letters in reply were lost in the war – it would have been difficult for my grandfather to retain personal papers as he travelled with his unit. But the surviving letters by Harold, and an additional letter from Jim, his brother-in-law, form a unique and personal record of the relationship between a husband and wife divided by war over eighty years ago.

Harold's letters reveal a stark contrast between the mundane minutiae of everyday issues, and the harsh, harrowing environment against which they are set. They give a glimpse of Joan's life too. Through his words, we get a sense of two people bound together with the underlying longing for hearth and home.

Karen Geraldine Croft

Harold (right) serving in the Home Guard before his conscription in 1941, aged 39

Cardoness
Gatehouse
Scotland. 2-4-34

H. Bishop
You will remember coming to see us
at Devilston in March, about the
situation of butler at Cardoness.
We can now definitely offer you the
situation of butler here from 1st October
if you can arrange to get temporary
employment until then.
We shall be away for part of May &
June and again in August & September
when house & shooting are likely to be let.
Your wages would be £80 a year with
cottage & coal – three or four tons depending
upon the size of the house you will occupy.
You would be given your own meals in
this house.
If in the meantime you find yourself
suited we can quite understand. ✱
Yours faithfully
_____ Hannay. (Col)

Harold's offer of employment at Cardoness House

INTRODUCTION

HAROLD BISHOP

Harold was an only child, born in Liverpool in 1902. When he was a small boy, his father left his wife and son to make his fortune in Australia. Harold's mother Marion was forced to provide and fend for the two of them on her own.

As a young man Harold began his first job, aged 16, to train as a footman at St James's Palace. His first appointment was at Belbroughton House near Bromsgrove, Worcester and his career in service continued apace. Following an interview with Colonel Rainsford-Hannay, Harold accepted the position of butler at Cardoness House near Gatehouse of Fleet, Dumfries and Galloway in 1934.

The Old Lodge was provided as accommodation. He was in charge of the serving staff: three people in the kitchen, three people in the pantry, three people in the house and two or three additional domestic staff.

Harold used his generous tips from guests to buy an Austin Seven. He was a very fit and athletic man, a great sportsman. He began by serving in the Home Guard, but he was conscripted to the army at the ripe old age of 39 and left Cardoness in September 1941 to begin his training at Redford Barracks in Edinburgh.

MARGARET JOAN BISHOP

Joan was born in High Hoyland near Barnsley, South Yorkshire in 1911 where her father, Herbert Roper, was a gamekeeper. Along with her mother Margaret Roper, sisters Doris and Brenda, and brother Jim, she spent her childhood moving around various estate lodges ending up at Sand Hutton.

Although Joan was extremely bright and passed the entrance exam to attend grammar school, she was destined to go into service at Sand Hutton Manor near Claxton, North Yorkshire where she met her future husband, Harold.

While Harold was away Joan was very worried that she and her little girls would be evicted from the Old Lodge. Therefore to keep her home she worked at Cardoness House as a temporary cook and housekeeper and lived in when required to do so. She described herself as a Yorkshire Lass and often said that the 11 years spent at Cardoness were the happiest of her life.

Young Joan

JAMES LESLIE ROPER

Jim was born in 1913 and grew up alongside his sisters Doris, Joan and Brenda. On leaving school he was employed at Sand Hutton Manor as a gardener but his dream was to join the navy. Upon conscription he became one of the 15 man crew on HM Strathborve as a stoker. The Aberdeen fishing trawler was requisitioned by the Royal Navy and converted to a minesweeper in 1940. On 6 September 1941 the vessel was struck by a German laid mine and sank off the Humber. Jim's body was never found.

His death is commemorated with an inscription on Lowestoft Naval Memorial, Panel 7 Column 1 that reads:

Stoker James Leslie Roper Service Number LT/ KX 121734 Royal Naval Patrol Service H.M Trawler Strathborve Died 06 September 1941 Age 28 years old Additional Info Son of Herbert and Margaret Roper; husband of Dorothy Roper of Skellow, Adwick-le-Street, Yorkshire

Jim and his wife Dorothy

POST CARD

THE ADDRESS TO BE WRITTEN ON THIS SIDE

12 SEP 1941

Mrs H. Bishop
Old Lodge
Cardoness
Gatehouse of Fleet
Castle Douglas

1130250. Gnr Bishop. H.
79 Squad 'A' Battery
38 Signal Training Regt. R.A.
Artillery Barracks.
Bedford
Edinburgh. 13.

Thur night

Dear all
Arrived safely. feeling
not too bad. Hope you are
all OK. I shall not be out.
for 7 days. Here for 5 months
So cheerio for now will
write letter soon. love
to all Yours Harold.

P.S. Get Cigs. from.
Clelland.

Harold's first letter home

THE LETTERS

12 September 1941

1130250 Gnr Bishop H
79 Squad. 'A' Battery
38 Signal Training Regt R.A.
Artillery Barracks
Redford
Edinburgh

Thurs night

Dear all

Arrived safely. Feeling not too bad. Hope you are all OK. Shall not be out for 7 days. Here for 5 months so cheerio for now. Will write letter soon. Love to all.

Yours Harold
P.S. Get cigs from Clelland.

NATIONAL SERVICE (ARMED FORCES) ACT 1939

All men aged 18 to 41 had to register for National Service. Harold was 39 years old.

The 38th Signal Training Regiment covered training in signalling (radio, flags and heliograph) and communications, driving motorcycles and vehicles, vehicle maintenance and knowledge of internal combustion vehicles. The training lasted 5 to 6 months.

The Royal Regiment of Artillery – Royal Artillery (RA) – is the artillery arm of the British Army.

Motto: *Ubique Quo Fas Et Gloria Ducunt*

Harold's Royal Regiment of Artillery service badge

Harold's Record of Service

Darling

I expect you have got my card saying I arrived OK also the things I did not require have been sent. I put the cap badge in for Cochrane. It is a very long and tiresome journey to Edinburgh. Have to change 3 times. I got into a carriage at Dumfries with an artillery man so got hold of a few tips also a few recruits got in. You tell them by their faces, some of them poor down at heel fellows but with their wives seeing them off all with the same feeling. However, we brightened up on the way then the spirits damped down again on nearing Edinburgh. However, here we are and unless we get kicked out have just to make the best of it. I must say I have been lucky in getting in a decent Squad so that helps enormously. I have made a couple of pals. One is an Edinburgh chap so when we get going things will not be too bad. This regiment is as strict and particular as the guards and reckon to turn you out as something super human. The first month is just Hell! when they hope to knock the rawness out of you. I actually started in 'A' Battery this morning. Had the first inoculation on Friday and get the next one on Tuesday then I get 48 hrs off but of course not allowed out of barracks. Everybody is fine over this Y.C.B which every recruit gets. The off time is very poor here at any time. 3 evenings a week from 6.30 pm and one afternoon a week. There is bags of food but of course rough. I think I get my educational test next week so I am praying I will pass. If you do not pass the tests you suffer. My boil has been playing me up a bit. It has not burst yet! I have not reported sick yet and don't want to if I can possibly help it as I don't want to miss anything as heaven knows it will take me all my time to pass with my thick head. My toe is getting on nicely and I have been able to rest it by wearing my gym shoes whenever possible.

Well, I have told you lots of things but you can ask me anything you want to know when you write. These are the largest barracks I have seen. In fact, they are the largest in the country I believe.

Oh, I am enclosing a card. Now if you have not heard from the Post Office regarding your pay send the card right away. It is all ready to hand to the postman. If you have heard from the P.O keep the card in a safe place as you may need it at a future date. Well, how are you getting on? I hope you are alright at nights and Marion's cold is better. I hope you got some cigs off Clelland as they say it is hard to get any in Edinburgh! There is a Naafi in the barracks but they are just letting you have 10 just now so expect they will conk out at any time. Now you will not get much washing, only vests which we are not supposed to wear. Also, I want to send my army socks to you to wash for the first time as they are two sizes too large at present but I will have to wait and see how I can wangle it for the kit inspection. Will you send my pyjamas as soon as you can? You can send both pairs if you like. You could put my name on but not my number. Well, I shall have to close now as it will soon be tea parade so hope this finds you well. My love and kisses to you all. I hope plenty of shrimps have been caught.

Cheerio.
Yours Harold
Xxxxxx

P.S. Be sure you write the address right. They are very particular about that. 1130250 Gnr Bishop H etc etc.

Dear Joan and Harold

Thanks ever so much my dears for the cake, it arrived in perfect condition.

As you will note by the address I am now at the main base and have started instruction in firing and on Diesel Engines. I don't know where I shall be sent to from here, it may be Patrol Boats, Motor Torpedo Boats, Minesweeping or the heavier class but we are pretty sure to be at sea within a fortnight.

I am on Police Patrol again tonight and have the afternoon off duty and am getting a few letters written.

I am in billets here, with a private family and it is a grand home; plenty of good food, a feather bed of all things and everything spotlessly clean; the only snag is I'm 2 and a half miles from the barracks (or land ship). We start at 9 am knock off for dinner at 12.30 pm, start again at 2.30 pm and finish for the day at 5 pm.

I'm in the very pink of condition, I think the navy was the life I was really cut out for.

I hope you can stay where you are if Harold is called up, it is not very nice splitting up your home as Dot can tell you.

I enjoyed my weekend very much, but it was too

short for us, and goodness only knows when I will have another leave. The enemy keeps on doing his stuff, I'm so used to hearing bombs and guns now that I feel quite lonely when they stop for a while; and he is doing some damage, believe me.

I hope the kiddies are in the best of health, give them a big hug from me and heaps of love and kisses.

I'll have to close now as I have two or three more letters to write before patrol at 4.30 pm.

So, lots of love, and keep smiling.
Your affect. bro.
xxxxxxxxxx Jim

Joan, Jim and Doris, 1914

Darling

Glad to hear you are all keeping OK and thanks for sending the parcel which I received alright. I am sorry to hear about Jim. It doesn't look too promising now but one never knows. It was a long time before news of Gordon got through. I wish Jim had not gone in for stoker. There is a little more chance above decks. Glad you got the pay doings alright. It is handy getting it every fortnight. I expect Mrs Spence is back and I suppose Peter is still waiting! Lucky dog. Well, I have been feeling pretty rotten after the last inoculation. It was a stunner. I was really ill after it and the 24 hrs off is just a damned twist. It only means off the physical part. The mental part goes on the same so we were at it until 6 pm our usual time. However, as soon as I got the chance, I went to the Naafi and got some aspros and a cup of tea and went back to bed. Well, I felt I had got double pneumonia. I could quite understand poor Jim going to hospital. Anyway, I stuck it out and am feeling better now apart from my arm feeling very sore when touched and my appetite has gone. The boil has faded almost away. Don't know what happened to it so expect the damn thing will come again unless these inoculations *[Incomplete]*

Darling

Thanks for the parcel and cigs. I was glad it came a bit early as I was wondering what would happen about my vest. Wednesday being my half day for the present I take the parcel down on that day to post it. They often change the arrangements. Thanks for Anne's letter. She seems to have got a decent job. You never said if Katie had gone back to the house. Neither the Col or Mrs Hannay came here. If it was Thurs or Friday, I had no pass out but they could have got in touch with me by going to the guard room. Of course, the Col should know all that. Now dear you don't say how you get on at nights so I hope that means you are alright. I wish the time would not drag with you. I'm glad to say it is going quickly with me for the days are so full and my head will have to swell double its size to take it all in. Of course, the trouble has lain with being buried for 7 years. I have come to the conclusion it is not good for one but don't you say anything there as we are definitely not finished there. Well, I got over the last inoculation on Sat better although my arm is still very sore. I went out to the sports and stayed out till they finished which I think is better to be out in the air than in bed. On Sunday we were on light duties until dinner time then finished so I spent the afternoon and evening on my bed studying so on Monday morning I did not feel so bad.

There is another devil to come yet and a vaccination. I have gone brown with the change of air and outdoor life but I expect it will wear off again after a week or two. Is Mrs Hampshire still staying on? I thought you said something about her not being suitable. Thank Marion for her nice letter and tell her Daddy is often thinking about her and wondering how she is getting on. On Thursday night I am on machine gun duty on the roof of the barracks so if there is an air raid I shall be in action for the first time.

Now you were asking if you should send any eats, well I don't think it is necessary really as we do get plenty, of course plain, but well cooked. I can wait for the fancy things when I come home. Oh, while I think of it will you send me a bit more carbolic soap in the next parcel. Now I am enclosing a pair of army socks as they make a mess of them at the laundry and I know how to work the kit inspection now. Now will you put my number on the little tab on the socks with the marking ink. Well dear I must close now so take care of yourself and let me know how you are getting on. Love and kisses to you all.

Ever yours
Harold
xxxxxx
I am enclosing a comic for Marion and Ann

Harold the footman

Darling

Thanks for yours but really dear it wasn't very helpful. I thought you were going to try and bear up. It would be such a help to me and it certainly is the best position we could be in. There is nothing like being sure of your home. Even if there was anywhere in Edinburgh it would be idiotic to come to live here as heaven knows where I will get posted to when I have finished here and I am sure you would not like to be left in Edinburgh so do try and be brave and stay where you are. It is every bit as bad for me. The only thing being the days are so full the time is going very quickly and of course the quicker they go the nearer to the end of my training so I shan't mind if they slow up a bit later on. Now dear it is almost a cert there will not be an invasion of this country. The next will be in the East. We are rapidly preparing for that now so I think you can have little fear as far as invasion goes. Well my dear, I hope you will save all you can towards the insurance. The premium is £3.18.6. Of course, there is a chance I shall be home before it is due which is the 31st December but what I was worrying about was not letting them know I was in the army. You see it will mean extra premium. On the other hand, if anything happens to me, I don't suppose you would get a penny and that would be all my hard earnings gone west. Anyway dear, we won't worry about it for a month or so. I shouldn't worry too much about the goings on at Cardoness. Just mind your business and don't do more than you can help. Glad the car is alright. Oh, I always forget to ask you if the reply came back from the insurance people. If not, it should be seen to. Darling I think I told you there wasn't much time off. One week there is two evenings, the next three evenings. That is after duty or after 6 pm. If you are on special duty such as guard, machine gun duty, orderly etc you lose whatever times going even the half day.

Well as I think I told you I don't bother about the evenings especially in this battery as I do "homework" until 10 pm most nights. I do like my half day when I can get it. I usually do odd jobs for myself, go to the town and post the parcel and sometimes go to the pictures. Sometimes one or two fellows come with me, sometimes I can't be bothered with anybody and go myself. Sometimes I end up in a canteen and answer my letters. Sometimes we get two Sundays out running and then not a Sunday for three weeks, it varies. I will be able to explain it better when I see you. I do not go out on Sunday unless I have somewhere definite to go. We are finished every Sunday by 12.30 pm whether we are out or not so it is an excellent chance for "homework" and I usually stick in all afternoon and evening. You can tell Marion her Daddy has lots of "homework" to do. Well Darling if there is anything else you want to know just ask me. No, I don't want my cardigan as I shall wear my gym pullover if necessary. Oh, Mr Ramsay saw me on Thursday, I don't think I told you. Mr Peck is adjutant here. He is a Captain. He used to come to Cardoness for tennis, well Mr Ramsay had come for tea with him. I had done 20 hrs on guard when he sent for me so naturally, I was feeling washed out. However, he didn't keep me long and was in rather an argumentative mood and as I was not feeling much better myself there was a pair of us. He said he was glad I did not go into his crowd. I said yes, I was more than pleased as I saw some on my way up. They can't even walk properly let alone march. Now dear I will leave this open until parcel arrives and finish it off then. Well dear I have just heard the squad are in barracks tomorrow so that means no half day and as I think I will be on guard again on Thursday I will try and get this off tonight if your parcel comes. It has not arrived yet. Now dear do try and bear up and keep my home going. It is the only thought that keeps my spirits up.

You know what happens to me if I lose heart so try and stick it.

You should be happy with those two little girls. Bye bye for now. All my love to you all.
Ever yours.
Harold
Xxxxxx

I managed to get a bar of choc from the Naafi. It is very little but make the best of it. No parcel has come so I will send this on in case I cannot get out until Friday.

I enclose my other new pair of army socks. Will you wash them and mark them with the number? Try and put a good piece of brown paper on parcel as I have to use it to send back. Can't get any here.

Darling

Thank you for the parcel which arrived this morning. I thought I had better send [my] letter on yesterday in case I cannot get out until Friday then you would have been wondering what had happened. If I am not on guard tomorrow, I will get it off then. If I am it will have to be Friday. Thank goodness it will only be 12 hour guard this time, the 24 hour is murder. Thank goodness my thick vest has come. We have not had our winter issue yet!! And this is the coldest spot I have ever been in. It snowed for about 20 minutes this morning. I hope the snow keeps off until this motor course is finished. Had my first taste of convoy driving yesterday and I got rather a shock as it is not so easy as it looks however, I got on not so bad. It was just a practise run as there is a big convoy run next week so I will let you know how I get on then and where we go. Tell Marion all the little boys and girls run out to wave to us the same as they do. Darling I do hope you are not going to have another boil. Do let me know how you are. I have kept clear so far, my behind has not been too good but I manage to keep going alright. Well Darling I must close now and get parcel ready then get on with some "homework". Thank Marion for her nice letter. Tell her Daddy is always thinking about her. Thank Jim Davidson for cigs. They are very welcome but I don't know why he should bother as I never had much to do with him. In fact, he is one I don't care for. Well bye bye darling. All my love to you all. Ever yours

Harold
Xxxxxx
P.S. Brenda sent me some cigs last week.

Joan with Jim Davidson at the nets in Laundry Bay (left)
Jim's parents, Mr and Mrs Davidson (right)

Joan's sister Brenda aged 20, 1944

29

My Darling

I have several letters to answer but I can't bring myself to answer any of them as I am in such awful pain but I thought I would like to start this to you. I can continue it tomorrow or Monday. My first suspicion was right. It is not a boil I have but a poisoned knee. I stuck it out till yesterday, Friday, as I was determined to sit the exam. They were very good about my driving test and let me through without going through it as they said I had been an excellent driver on the trials. I shall not know the result of the exam until the middle of next week. Well dear getting back to the point, this morning the poison had crept up to my groin so off I went to the M.O and had it opened up then I have been down to the sick bay four times for hot or I should say boiling fermentations and thank heavens I have had the last one till 9 am tomorrow. I am now on 10.C. that is excused all duties but the army is no place for a sick man if not in hospital which of course I did not want to happen as I don't want to be relegated. This week is dispatch riding course but obviously the M.O forbid me to go near a motorcycle. I don't know if I shall be fit enough by the end of the week but if I am not, I really won't be sorry as the test is terrific. Usually, half the fellows are brought back on stretchers. My nerve is not so good since I had the accident and messed my knee up. Well darling how are you feeling now. I do hope your ear is better and I hope that will be your last. They are such beastly painful things. I hope too you are sleeping better at nights and not so nervous. Marion is a big girl now and should be good company. I don't know when she will get her piano lessons. To think that there are all those pianos up at the big house and it would be fine if she could have practiced on one, but I suppose we will just have to wait and see what the end of this damned war will bring. It is terribly cold here again. It has been that sleety snow. I felt it more through not being active.

Well dear I have just got back from the M.O this morning and I think my knee is going on the right road. He said there was still a small septic spot and he said you have had a narrow escape. He will not have it that anything entered the knee. He said the start of it would be a boil. Well darling I am writing this in penny numbers. I hope you won't be bored as it seems mostly about my troubles. Darling I do seem to be unlucky. I thought my knee was getting on nicely but this morning the M.O was not pleased with it. He said he would give it 24 hrs and if there is not a great improvement by then he will have to operate. I seriously hope that will not have to be. It seems to be I have not to go on the motorbikes and I don't suppose you are sorry about that. Well dear I did not put my vest in last week as I thought I would wear it a fortnight like I do at home but if you think it is too dirty tell me and I will change every week. We have just been issued with the winter undies so I am sending the vest for you to wash. It looks big enough for a nightie

31

to me. It seems a long while since I heard from you. I used to like your surprise letters on Saturdays. Of course, this has been a long week and I have had no letters as I owe everybody one. I had a letter from my Aunt at Slough the other week. She was very sympathetic about you and sends her love. I will get someone to post the parcel tomorrow if yours comes today and if I have to have the operation, I will let you know in between. If you don't hear you will know I am getting on alright and will be passing out into 'C' Battery on Saturday. Will you send my other piece of Necco soap? I think it is in my wee case. I will have enough carbolic for another week, I think. Well darling the parcel hasn't come today. It does seem ages since I heard from you. I hope you are alright. Parcel just arrived but I will not be able to add much as tonight will be the best chance of getting this posted. Darling I was annoyed to hear you were going to live in the house. I know only too well what that means.

You will never get out. That big fat woman was never meant for work. Darling you must be at home when I come on leave. Oh, I think I should die if I had to come home to a home of emptiness. I couldn't come to that big house after this life and there are such a lot of things we have to talk over in the privacy of our own little home. Darling you must promise me to be at home when you hear definitely I am coming. It may be any time between now and Xmas and I definitely will not live or sleep at that big house so that is final with me. Darling I don't think I should have Marion inoculated. I think it is a lot of rot and I feel sure she will grow out of it. I was sorry to hear about Major McLellan. Darling my leg is bad. I know what the verdict will be when I go down. I would leave this until tomorrow to let you know but heaven knows when I should be able to get it away, so dear if you don't hear anything by Saturday you will know I am getting on alright and address the next parcel to 'C' Battery and do make it quite clear with Mrs H that you must be at home when I come.

So, bye bye for now.
All my love and kisses to you all.
Ever your
Harold

Thank Marion for her letter. Tell her Daddy's knee is very sore but he hopes it will soon be better and you can't see the place where we got tea on the card which of course was a canteen.

Have not heard the result of the exam yet. If you have got razor blades keep them. Put them in my wee case. I will let you know if I want them. I may be able to manage until I come home.

Bye bye.

I forgot to leave my socks off this morning and it is such agony to take them off so will send them next time.

Joan and Marion at Cardoness House
(The Big House), 1936

Cardoness House, 1930s

Darling

Thanks for the letter. It was a surprise as I did not expect one until the parcel. I am glad Ann liked her bag. Did she get any other presents? Well dear as you can see, I managed to scrape through. I failed hopelessly with the morse but I passed well with everything else. I will have to work hard on the morse at nights and try and level up. The pass out went without a hitch and I must say very good considering the mixed ages which ranges from 19 to 41. However, the Colonel was very pleased and we had the sergeant to thank. He is the best in the barracks. He certainly put us through hell but it was all for the good. The discipline of this battery is more strict but the course is motor engineering and driving so I will be in my element. I will let you know how I get on as I go along. There were just three fellows relegated. That means another fortnight for them in 'A' battery poor devils. Well dear I went round to see Thom on Sunday but he is away on a job. However, Mrs Thom was there and the son and I saw the daughter but I did not feel very comfortable so I got away as soon as possible. I had tea and buzzed off asking them to tell Thom to send me a card when he comes back. Of course, they lost no time in telling me 2nd Lt Rainsford Hannay and Colonel Gordon had paid a visit the day before. I thought the other daughter was the nicest but she was very busy with her fiancé also a doctor. They seem to be in a nice state at the house but for heaven's sake don't you take anything on. Did you get the broadcast? I didn't care much for the tunes of the band. I've heard them *[Incomplete]*

35

Darling

Thanks for yours of this morning. I was very worried about my leg too, but I am glad to tell you it is going on alright now, really a miracle happened which of course was not very nice for me or the M.O. at the time. He was preparing me for the knife and having a final mess about with it when all of a sudden it burst and spurted like a fountain. I shall never forget it. The M.O. was covered in blood which seemed to worry him but afterwards he said I'm glad that happened as it got the poison away better than he could have done it. I have had it dressed several times since and it is heavily bandaged. The awful swelling at the groin has gone so I think in a few days when it has healed over a bit, I shall be alright. Well darling I passed my drivers I.C so I am quite pleased with myself. I hate the beginning in the new Batterys and it gets harder and harder as we go on, however, I will let you know more in the parcel. I will get someone to post this today. Glad you are alright at nights now and hope you don't work too hard at the house. Might be able to give you definite news of leave in about a week's time. Will explain better in letter I will write tomorrow for parcel.

Bye bye.
All my love to you all.
Ever your
Harold
Xxxxxx

Darling

I am starting this today, Sunday, as I can't do anything else very well as I have to keep my leg up to rest it. I think all the poison is out at last but it doesn't feel right somehow and it is awfully weak. I do hope it is not going to be a trouble to me for the rest of my days. Well Darling I expect you are busy at the house now but I hope you are not doing the cleaning as well as the cooking for I know that is too much without any handicaps so do see they get someone in for the cleaning. And I hope you are getting your food alright, also plenty for the children. Well darling if everything goes alright, and I am praying it will, there is only 22 days to go and I shall be home. I'm afraid I have not got up to standard with the morse yet as I am still 2 words behind but of course I have been handicapped with my leg. I have missed several practice tests but I am trying very hard now to catch up, if only I can do it in this coming fortnight I shall be alright. I am glad to say I was better on the lamp today. On one test message I was 100%. Now Darling you asked me some time ago for a photo of myself, well here it is. I had it taken several weeks ago. In fact, it was just when my knee first started to function. Of course, it will have to do for your Xmas as I had to borrow money and I am paying it back a bit each week. I was going to keep it until Xmas but I thought perhaps you would rather have it now. I hope you will like it, the uniform is quite good and of course you will have seen those eyes somewhere else! Thanks for the parcel and letter. You seem to be very busy. It would be nice if you had a little to do to occupy your mind but I don't like you doing so much so I do hope you will be finishing soon. If you have a breakdown that will be the worst thing that could happen so if that big lazy woman doesn't get herself back soon you must tell her you can't go on. I think you should be at home a week at least before I come for your own sake.

Poor Marion taking sandwiches in this winter weather. I do think it is a shame. I hope she gets something very substantial when she comes in at night. I was unable to get the parcel off on Tuesday and the squad was in on Wednesday so I had to get someone to post it on Thursday. It doesn't matter about the pants being marked as I shall be putting them on tomorrow so I can hardly have them pinched off my back. You did not mark the vest last time so I am wearing that one now and perhaps you can manage to mark it next time in not quite such a conspicuous place if you can help it. I had a nice letter from Harold again. He has offered to lend me some money to pay the insurance, however I wrote and told him I would wait until I got home to talk it over with you. Of course, I hope we can manage to pay it ourselves. I hope she pays you well for your work there. Hilda is back in Birmingham so they are all together again at a new address but I expect you will have heard from them. Well dear my knee is better than it was but it is not right yet. It feels as if there was still something in it and you remember the toe the horse tramped on, well it has started to get very sore. If that is going to start now, I think I shall go potty. Thank Marion for her letter. I think she is a clever girl to write by herself. I am wondering how they are up all those stairs by themselves when you are down doing the dinner. It's a wonder they are not frightened. Well Darling I must stop now and get the parcel done up and I am going to try and manage down with it myself to the post as I want to get some fresh air so bye bye for now. All my love and kisses to you all. Ever yours Harold Xxxxxx

Sorry to hear Angus has not got what he wanted. Of course, I don't see how he could have done anything else as he is handicapped with his eye and his temperament wouldn't stand any brain work.

This is Harold's address:
73 Birchwood Crescent
Mosely
Birmingham 13.

Are you sending them anything for Xmas? I will be sending a card. I have some regimental ones. I could send them one of those photos but I don't think anybody appreciates them and it is such a waste so let me know if you are sending something. I will just send a card. Funny place for Ramsay to be going just now but that is the army all over. The red tape makes me sick. The influx of recruits now are all youngsters. I think they have realised the difficulty of ramming this stuff into the heads of older men. I am the only Englishman in this squad now and not a 100% one at that so the squad is 99.5% Scotch with the exception of the I.V.C.Os of course who are all English. The Sgt belongs to Liverpool. Cheerio for now. Take care of yourself.

H.

Harold and Hilda (friends of Harold and Joan)

Predecessors at the Old Lodge, the Thom family

Darling

Thank you very much for the parcel and shortbread. I will get it divided out.

I wish you had thought and put my thick vest instead of my other one. It is bitterly cold here now and we have not had our winter issue yet.

Wish we could have brought our sergeant from 'A' battery. He used to get our things in no time. Anyway, if you will send me a thick one next time as I will send you one to be washed and aired when we do get them.

Well dear I am getting on not so bad. Have been driving the very big lorries like you see go by in the convoys. As for the other part I am getting on slowly but there are such a lot of technical words to remember and tons of brain work. I am working every night until 10 o'clock.

It must be a rum place the house now. I can imagine Mrs Rainsford. I have not written to them. Can't seem to find time and the money doesn't run to many 2 half pennies. Anyway, I don't think it is really necessary, do you?

Well dear I am not sure when I shall get the parcel off as I am on main gate guard which is a 24 hour guard so I shall not be off until 6 pm tomorrow, Wednesday, however I might get an hour off on Thursday. If not, I will get someone to post it.

We had this photo taken before we left 'A' battery.

Now take care of it as I have got most of the fellows'

signatures. They were the officers of 'A' battery and the sergeant is sitting on their right, Sgt Major on their left.

I am sending one of these to your mother.

[Incomplete]

'A' Battery Squadron, Harold is marked with an arrow

My Darling

Thanks for the letter and thank Marion for hers. I am glad she liked her present and tell her Daddy thinks the transfer is very nice. She does them quite well now. Yes darling, I often feel just as lonely but I find it best to say nothing and keep my chin up as much as possible because I know nothing can be done about it and for how long it will go on for I just don't try and think but pray for the day when it is all over and we are all together again. I too often think of the nice times. We had wonderful times really. I like to think when I go to bed at night when there is a peaceful hour or two. I not only think of the pleasant days before we were married but of the past nine years. I have no regrets. Perhaps Darling there will be some more of those years to come for us.

What I would like first would be a little "honeymoon" perhaps just a few hours just you and I somewhere nice. We will have to see what we can do about it. I knew you would hear from Mrs Spence. In fact, it was me who told her to write and ask you to come. I don't know how she could say I was looking fit for I was anything but. Even strangers were remarking how ill I looked however darling on my last cig and not one to be had anywhere round here. Your parcel of last week must have been hung up somewhere and I had a job to get yours off as the P.O closes at 6.30 here and we are not finished till that time but as it happened, I had to go on a truck to the other side of Glasgow so I posted your parcel in Glasgow. Well darling I feel pretty certain it will be Friday we start leave so if you do not hear anymore, I shall be home either Friday night or Saturday morning. I hope you can get away from the house before Thursday darling as it won't give you much time. Don't bother about the garden dear I will do it while I am at home. I won't send my towel in case there is a kit check before we go so maybe you could give it a rinse through when I come. Now I am posting this today Saturday so you should get it on Monday. Bye bye for now. All news when I see you. All my love to you all. Ever yours Harold Xxxx

Darling

I must start this tonight for if the parcel comes tomorrow, I shall have to get yours off as the squad is in on Wednesday. We just get every other Wednesday and every other Sunday in this battery. If your parcel doesn't get here tomorrow it will mean Thursday before I can get yours posted. Well dear I am still hanging on by a slender thread and still struggling to get up to standard. Also, another slender thread has attached itself with the damn Japs starting but I don't think that will make any difference to us for a while and I am still hoping to be home a fortnight today. Could you get a chicken for Xmas day? Do try. Perhaps it would be time enough to order it next week when you are more sure I am coming. That's of course if you were not already having one for yourselves! I hope that woman has got back so you can get a rest. My knee is getting on nicely. I think all the poison is out. It is still heavily bandaged but I have fixed it so I can walk. I have two dirty hankies this week as I have had an awful cold. It was a job struggling with these tiny hankies however I managed, escaping with a very sore nose. We have certainly got our backs to the wall now and unless America does something big, we shall be at it for years if we don't collapse in the attempt.

It has been terribly cold here again although it is seldom anything else. It is the coldest spot I have been in and the barracks are right on top of a hill, however I suppose it is much healthier than being down in Edinburgh itself. Thanks for the parcel which only arrived by second post today. I suppose there is a rush on at the P.O. which is making them later in coming. Thanks for the shortbread. It will be greatly appreciated. The food here has dropped down a peg lately. The cigs got squashed a bit in the bag.

Doesn't Clelland give boxes or packets anymore? However, they will smoke alright. I am glad that big fat woman is coming back and don't you go up when she is back. I think you were daft to do the cleaning as well. There are plenty of women she could have got in for that. Now dear it wasn't the week for the vest last week and you said once a fortnight would do. I am still struggling with the morse. I am fed up with the damn thing and a 101 other things to memorise too, however I can keep my head above water. I shall be home on Monday week 22nd. There is to be a preliminary exam on Saturday so that will seal my fate. Well Darling I will close now. Don't send my pyjamas or vest unless I write and tell you but send cigs, hankies and socks. Bye bye for now. Love you all. Ever your Harold Xxxxxx

My own Darling

As you will see I got back safely but I shall never forget the journey as long as I live. The train at Lockerbie was 2 hours late. What a wait. I was frozen to the bone, then when it did come in the sides were literally bulging. I've never seen anything like it. I had to fight my way in and just stay put. By the time we got to Carstairs my back was almost in two. I did not get here until 10.45 pm so I was thankful we went into that little place for a cup of tea before I left Dumfries. I hope you got back alright. Darling I wished afterwards I had kept my pack nearer the bus stop so as I could have seen you off. Now sweetheart I must thank you for the lovely time you gave me. I enjoyed every minute of it and you worked hard, so hard to make things nice for me only the time went too quickly. However, I feel the time will go quickly then I will be seeing you again. Well darling I would like to get this off to you so I'm afraid I will have to cut it short. I had the lovely surprise last night to see my name up for guard tonight which piled the agony on still more. Thank God it is the 12 hrs one as my head is just splitting. I had a very nice letter and card from my other

Aunt. I will send them next time for you to read along with the other bits of news so bye bye Darling.

Take great care of yourself.
All my love and kisses to you all.
Big kisses for Marion and Ann xx
Ever your
Harold
Xxxxxx

Harold, Marion and Ann

My own darling

Thanks for the cigs and letters but I will not send this until you send washing and then we will get straight again. I shan't be writing to that person as of course I won't be going. It certainly wouldn't be worth it on a half day when you know nothing about the people. Well Darling you must have been wishing very hard for they have come true! My name has gone through to be posted to the field. I must say I am feeling pretty down in the mouth about it not because I want to go against your wishes but because I feel sure there has been some underhanded work going on for I did not even get the chance of relegation. However, I am going to see what I can do. I might write to Col. John and I will see Pick and try and get back on the motors at the same time pushing my own job forward. Oh, I don't know I'm sure it's such a hell of a job getting anything altered in the army once it has gone through. Now you will have got my letter in the parcel telling you what I did on New Year's Eve. I was on duty on fire picket. There was an awful to do about New Year's Day with these Scotsmen as they quite got it into their heads they would get off from the Weds evening till Friday morning. Instead, they only got Weds evening up to the usual time so of course there was a riot. I got a pass to go out New Year's Day as I missed Weds evening. My Aberdonian friend broke barracks with somebody else's pass so we went to the pictures.

Three others broke barracks and two were caught so they are now serving GB and were stopped a day's pay. On Sunday I went to find that distant relation of mine but she was out so I adjourned to a canteen and wrote to my aunt and Brenda. Had something to eat and came back. I am going to see my relation on Saturday evening, if I am still here! I am glad your colds are almost better. I hope Ann will keep clear of it. I have had an awful dose.

I could have done with another dozen hanks however I managed by drying them off. My big toe is very sore apart from that it is alright. The frost plays the devil with it. I am keeping elastoplast on so it shouldn't get poisoned. I was relieved to hear you can stay in the lodge and don't have to go to the house permanently. I hope Mrs McMath doesn't send any scones because the fellows wouldn't thank you for them without butter. Glad you were able to get cigs. I hope you will be able to get some more this weekend. Darling if I don't hear from you in the morning, I will send this as you might not send it until the weekend. Well darling nothing from you today so I will post this tonight. Oh, the scones have arrived plus some butter so I will distribute as many as I can. If you see her will you thank her. I suppose I will have to drop her a line later. Now Darling I will let you know immediately anything definite happens so bye bye for now. All my love to you all. Ever yours Harold Xxxxx

The cake was very good indeed Darling.

My own Darling

Thanks for parcel. I am glad it came today as there is a kit check tomorrow morning. I am worried about you again as I thought your nervousness was going to leave you. I do wish these daft people wouldn't come knocking at night. I have no doubt it being McCormack on his New Year stint. I don't think anyone outside the estate would come and I notice nothing happened while I was at home so darling, don't let your imagination run away with you too much. I shall be thankful when the lighter nights come. I am sorry about the wireless darling. I wish I could have got a H.T battery before I left and fixed it up for you, for I think that is the trouble although I am not quite sure of the small ones. I don't think they are being charged very well. You might get the other one from McMath and ask him if it is fully charged. If so, put it on and if it should fade out in a night or two well it is definitely the H.T. battery. I ordered one from McMurray so call sometime and see if it is in. I don't know how you will go about fixing it up. If only I had thought I could have marked the wires for you. If you do attempt it be sure the wireless is switched off before connecting the new battery and don't switch it on until all plugs are securely in their sockets or you will blow all the valves. You will see how the old battery is tapped by the holes. The black lead with black plug which runs from the switch goes in the negative that is the hole marked – and the red plug in the positive marked + and I think there is a plug on a white lead goes next 100 or 110. I tell you what, if you mark them yourself with bits of sticky paper before you disconnect the old battery you can't go wrong. I do hope you will manage. I was relieved to hear you got home alright but you assured me you were going to be brave you naughty girl.

I could see wee Marion was pretty full when I said goodbye bless her but darling the weeks will soon slip by and I shall be seeing you all again. I am still jogging along. Not much improvement but I am only just beginning to get shipshape again as I have been kept at it giving me little time for thought for as I told you my name was up for guard on Tuesday night and Wednesday night I was on fire picket so I am hoping to get a damn good sleep tonight. You remember I told you about Shand the duffer of the squad at morse, well his greeting was to be posted. He goes to Dalry on the guns tomorrow. It was a blow of course as he is an Edinburgh man. So now I am left the duffer so we will see. I will try and stick here as long as I can for your sake. My learned friend has strained his heart and is on the sick list and I think he is trying to work his ticket on the strength of it, so that's that. Of course, if he does go, I could still keep in touch with him. Darling when I was in the bath this evening my big toenail came right off. It is very sore and funny looking. I have put a bit of Elastoplast over it so hope it will be alright. If there is a route march tomorrow I must try and get out of it. You did not mention anything about the big house. I was relieved. I hope you will be able to stay in the wee lodge in peace then the light nights will soon be here and you will give up the thought of wanting to get nearer to me for I will probably be in a restricted area if I am in this country which would be just as big a disappointment for you. Oh, I heard from Mr Ash and I am enclosing the receipt as I might lose it here so put it in my wee case. I managed to get a bit of choc from the Naafi for the children and have some yourself darling. Well bye bye for now and I do hope you won't get any more scares. With all my love to you all and lots of kisses.

Take care of yourself and I hope your cold will soon be better.
Ever yours
Harold Xxxxxx
X just for yourself

Redfad

Darling

Do not send parcel as I
am leaving Edinburgh on Monday
don't know where to but will
let you know as soon as I can
I will profably post some things
on to you tommorow for to keep
at home. but I will try and put
a wee note in. Bye Bye for now
my love to you all.

Ever yours
Harold xxxx

Darling

I am just starting these few lines. It is 8.30 and I have just managed to get a bed of sorts together. I managed to get here alright but what luck I have darling I found I had lost both the passes. I think I must have left them at Craig's surgery. Luckily, I brought that letter they sent me or I should probably have been kept in the guard room for the night. Well, my darling I'm afraid I am feeling very wretched and lonely. The whole of the squad is away. Some have gone to various parts of England and some to the Orkneys. Darling I'm afraid I can't write very much more tonight as I must go and see if I can get something hot to drink as my throat is parched. I will not post this until tomorrow as I might know something definite by then. I did hate leaving you all on the station darling. Do take great care of yourself for me. Darling I heard tonight that the whole 79 squad with the exception of my learned friend and Tommy Thackeray are overseas so you will be glad I did not pass the signallers. Darling I can't put any address anyway until the morning as I am still attached to C Battery but I will probably be transferred to Depot in the morning and I expect shall have to wait for the next draft but I am not sure. I hope you are feeling better Darling and your pain has gone and do let me know when you are not well. I hope you won't have to go into the hospital for a long time and not at all if you can keep well without going. Don't go to work at the house under any pretext for I feel it is too much of a strain and that brings your trouble on.

Friday morning

Darling I have just been down to the office and I go to Depot Battery in the morning. I shall be here for a few days yet as I am to be vaccinated on Tuesday. I hope that won't knock me out again.

I have put in for my proficiency pay but I don't know how long it takes to get through. I am feeling very dithery this morning but I will give myself until the morning and if I don't feel better, I will report sick but I am hoping to shake it off. Well Darling I hope I can catch the post so as you will get it in the morning so bye bye for now. All my love to you all.

Ever yours Harold
Xxxxx

Troop 2
2nd Reserve Field Regt. R.A.
Billet 32 Waterloo Rd
Thursday   Nottingham
England.

My Darling
            We did not travel
until yesterday morning so
did not arrive till 7.30 last
night. No idea how long I
shall be here. Well I must
get this off as I need my
washing and it will be
a devil these next few day
getting into this. Bye Bye
for now darling all my
love Ever Yours
            Harold
            xxx

59

Joan and Marion

Ann outside the 'wee lodge' with the same teddy

My own darling

Thanks for your letter and cake. I have not cut it but I will take it down for tea today. So glad to hear your colds are better and you have got the wireless going again. I had my suspicions all along it was the L.T batteries. Don't be in a hurry to get a new H.T battery but if you have a chance of one later on take it and keep it in a dry place. The other one might last until I get home again. I am glad to hear they are getting fixed up at the house but they must be poor objects if they can't truss a bird! I am glad Marion got to the concert. I expect she would enjoy it. Glad we got Emily and Jacks address right. I made out as much as I could of her letter. She is such a funny writer isn't she. Your mother's letter was here when I got back from leave and I got a letter from Brenda the next day and I have answered them both. There is just one owing to my Aunt in Slough which I will send when I am in a better mood. I went to see my mother's cousin yesterday evening and enjoyed my visit very much. There was such a lot to talk about and learn. She put herself out to make me comfortable and I think I ate her weeks rations. She just lives alone with I think she said an Aunt! An old girl about 80 who I never saw so their rations are scanty. I wish I could get her some eggs. She does love them and only gets 1 a month and sometimes that one is bad. It is so pathetic. She is very like my Mother especially her speech so much that sometimes I thought it was Mother I was talking to and Darling, this is not my first visit to

Edinburgh! My Grandmother took me to that very same house and I sat at the same table when I was very young and I cannot remember a thing about it. From what I can fathom I must have been between 6 and 7 when I went. It's funny how some things go completely out of one's mind.

My aunt in Southport never mentioned any of her troubles in her letters but I learned her house in Wallasey was levelled to the ground and the one they are in now at Southport caught the blast of bombs last week and not a pane of glass or a breakable thing inside the house was left whole. She has gone away for a week or two a bag of nerves. Darling whatever you do stick in that little lodge as long as you can. I can feel you are at least safe. So, when it enters your head about getting near where I am, think of the risk of Marion, Ann and me. My eldest cousin who lives in Suffolk has no family. My younger cousin who lives in Southport near his mother has two of the loveliest children, a boy and a girl. The girl looks about the same age as Marion and the boy a bit younger than Ann. I think I have lost both my other cousins the sons of my other aunt. They were in the Merchant Navy. I don't know if they were both on the same boat or not, however they have both gone such fine lads too. So much for the news of my relations which I learned from my mother's cousin. I expect your bored stiff by now. Well darling it is time I got down to brass tacks as you will see I go to Depot Battery in the morning. That is the first stage of my transfer. I was in front of the Colonel this morning. I am fully convinced now some dirty swine has shot my bolt but I may find out before I leave. From what I can fathom I may be here for a fortnight yet. I'm afraid Darling your visit to Edinburgh will have to be treated as a myth for the time being. I cannot express my feelings. I am sure of being here one week at least as the Colonel wants me to look after him while his batman is on leave. That may lead to opportunities. We will see. For the time being you sit dumb darling. Now darling I will have to close and get packed up to go to Depot Battery in the morning. I got paintbrushes for the children. I got two for Marion a fine one and a thick one the other for Ann but I hope they will take care of them as they were rather expensive but will last a long time.

I am glad you sent some Elastoplasts as I use a lot for my toe as I have to put a fresh piece on every time I bath. I have an awful bad cough which keeps me awake nearly all night. I got some Veno's yesterday. I hope it will take it away. Well bye bye for now.

All my love to you all.
Ever your
Harold
Xxxxxx

My Darling

Yours to hand this morning. I am glad you wrote before sending cigs but I do hope you send them tomorrow or it will mean I shall have to buy and I have very little money as I got nothing for the week I was at home. Also, they made a mistake with the last weeks giving me 2/6 less however I suppose I will manage somehow. I am glad you are feeling better but I do wish you would not get such pains. You must not go on and ignore them for that may mean you being very ill later on so darling do take care. I am feeling better than I did and I think I have shaken the "flu" off but I have still got a nasty cough which keeps me awake at night not that I need much keeping awake for I don't sleep very much anyway. Strange as it may seem in the next bunk to me is another Aberdonian so I have attached myself to him. He has been transferred here from the "Scottish Horse" to go before a medical board for some peculiar reason best known to themselves. However, he is hoping to be degraded C.3. and get his ticket. Also, on the same bunk as him is a L/Bombardier also from the "Scottish Horse". A bit better class and educated so quite good company to be next to which makes me happier than I was. He is here on a similar footing as my Aberdonian friend. He has an awful skin disease on his legs which he blames the blankets or the khaki cloth for. I am wild at losing my blankets. I don't like these things I have now and I always have the feeling someone dirty has owned them. However, I shall have to put up with them now, I expect for the rest of my days in the army which I hope will be few. I did not get vaccinated today. They have prolonged the agony until tomorrow morning at 10.30. I shall be glad when it is over. I have a feeling I am going to take it badly. Yes, I went to the Spences with the Meccano bits on Sunday. We get a half day on Sunday in Depot Battery so naturally I grabbed the chance.

They were quite nice. I half expected to find them out but they were sitting in the window like a couple of love birds. I had a grand bath and she baked cakes for the tea. He gave me some books to take back with me which I find is a great help. I got the wind up terribly coming back for every bus was packed and would not stop. Spence was very good. Raced with me on cars to different bus stops and eventually got on one. I put in for a pass but I did not get it. However, that's taught me a lesson. I would not go again without one. Spences will think I'm a damn nuisance all round. Darling it was a blessing you did not come to Glasgow for the very week you were coming an epidemic of measles broke out. Douglas did not get a proper dose but got German measles, she said, but it's funny he has been off school 3 weeks. Well Darling I shall be here a week yet as I am on P.A.D. duty until next Tuesday morning. I will try and get my washing off on Thursday but I have no brown paper and I don't know if I will manage to get out before the shops close but I will try and get some somewhere.

When I go I will send you a wire so be cautious before you send washing back again. I think now I shall have to wait for the next draft which may be a fortnight yet, but so long as you don't get a wire you will know I am still here. Now darling they give me the rank of driver now so you must address me as Dvr instead of Gnr. I think the proficiency pay will be through next week. I am not quite sure how they work it yet, but I heard you might get it all, poor me, however I will be able to tell you for sure next time. Well Darling I must close now so do take great care of yourself. All my love to you all.

Ever yours
Harold
xxxx
Hope the car is alright.
Send cigs soon

THE SCOTTISH HORSE

The Scottish Horse was a Yeomanry Regiment of the British Territorial Army from 1902 to 1956. It carries the traditions and battle honours of The Scottish Horse raised in South Africa in 1900 for service in the Second Boer War. The regiment saw heavy fighting in World War II as part of the Royal Artillery.

My Darling

Well, I have had a hellish few days. What with the rush and long journey from Scotland and now I am on a 24 hour guard. I will not get back till 6 o'clock tonight and I am hoping to find your parcel there when I get back, for I have a feeling I shall not be here long for there is something in the wind. Darling it was a terrible feeling of longing came over me when the train stopped at Dumfries. A thought struck me you might have been at the station. Quite mad of course but how lovely to have seen you for those few minutes. However, my desire was satisfied when we steamed out 10 minutes to twelve. I knew then it was impossible for you to be there. I think I will like a service unit better when I get used to it. Of course, it is much harder work and more responsibility. If Dorothy and Jim had been at Derby still, I might have managed to see them but as it stands there is nobody I know within miles. However, it doesn't matter for all the time I shall be here. Well my darling I hope you and my little girls are quite well and everything is alright. Now you should be getting 3s/9p a week more now, that is 2s for the children and 1s/9p of my proficiency pay. We get half each. So if you are not getting it let me know. I wish the damned war was over but heavens it seems to get more serious. In fact, I am beginning to wonder if everything is going to be in vain. Will you get some razor blades when you get a chance? Well darling I will leave this till I get yours. Oh, I am putting this tin of corned beef and tin of milk in. They will come in useful. I was supposed to hand them in as subsistence rations however they didn't get there. Sunday: Darling isn't it awful.

The Battery P.O was closed when I came off duty last night and it is closed all day today so I can't get my parcel and I do long for news of you and I've no cigs and my pants and towel are filthy. Tomorrow is Bank Holiday so I expect the P.O will be closed and I shall probably be on guard again so goodness knows when I will get your parcel off. We will have to try and get it worked to the middle of the week again then if I should be on the 24 hour guard I will get it the next day. Well, my darling I will leave this open till tomorrow and if I have time to add a bit more, I will do so but if I see a chance to get a post I will take it. You will note by address I have moved next door and I forgot to put the Battery on your last letter. Darling I have just received parcel. What luck. I also received cigs but it is not safe to send cigs that way here so I think perhaps it will be better to get them in the parcel and darling do try and get more paper as it was all torn and the string hanging off. You see darling I left Bonhill at 7.30 am so Weds post would not have arrived so really my will was in vain as I was reckoning on you posting it on Wednesday as usual, however it was my fault for telling you to send it quickly. The post from here must take double the time as I posted your letter on Thursday morning. Darling I wish you hadn't to go to hospitals at all. It does worry me although I expect this will help to cure you. Anyway, I hope so. It looks as if Mrs R.H is beginning to smell a rat but I do hope you will be able to stop for the summer after putting in that awful winter. Of course, you certainly must not go to the house to work. It would be very awkward with the car if they turned you out, however we had better look on the brighter side of things just at present. Well, my darling I must finish this now. As I suspected no P.O open today being Bank Holiday so I will do my best to get it off tomorrow (Tuesday).

I see my name is not up for guard but I am going out on a scheme so God knows how long that will take. Probably the whole day but I do hope I shall be back in time to get the P.O open. I am driving a monkey/wireless truck. If you look in my book at the page I was explaining to you, you will see the position I will be taking. It will be marked M.I and I think in the second group. I hope I shall be alright, probably a bit nervous for the first time in charge of a vehicle. Don't send any money darling as I get half (1s/9d) of the proficiency pay and I know you can do with all you can get. Bye bye for now and thank Marion for her letter and tell her I will probably find more time to write to her next time. All my love to you three. Ever yours.

Harold Take care of yourself darling
Xxxxxx

LEAVE OR DUTY RATION CARD

(14 Days)

9

NAVY, ARMY AND AIR FORCE

1. Holder's Name ..... *Bishop. A.* .....

   Rank..... *Gunner* ..... No. *1130250*

2. Unit or Ship ..... 243rd Battery
   51st (H.) ANTI-TANK REGT. R.A.

3. Leave or { Beginning.. *24.5.42* .....
   Duty   { Ending ..... *31. 5. 42* .....

4. Signature and Rank }
   of Officer Issuing } *Major, R.A.*

5. Unit or Ship of }
   Officer Issuing } *Battery. R.A. (s.s.t.)*

Serial No. **WH** 709384

R.B.S.
(53935-1) 11,000M.

71

My darling

I am starting this today hoping yours will arrive soon. I am wondering if you have been to the hospital yet, if so, I hope you got over the ordeal alright and you are feeling better. It seems an awful long time to wait for your news now. It looks as if we can't do it under a week however I suppose we must be thankful for that and hope it won't get any worse. I was wondering if it would be a better idea if you sent your letter separate. I should know then your parcel was in the post. Of course, it would mean extra expense which I don't want you to have however I will leave it to you to do what you think best. Well darling I got over the scheme business alright. Managed the driving part alright but made a mess of things on the scheme itself. Would have been blown to pieces had it been the real thing. However, a good cursing done me no harm and I shall know better the next time. It was an imaginary invasion of Nottingham, quite interesting really. I like a service unit much better than a training unit. The days are more interesting but I wish they would interest and finish altogether so I could come home. Darling, I had my first experience under canvas last Thursday. Unfortunately, it was very cold and windy and poured with rain at times so my first impression was not good but I think in the middle of summer it would be ideal so I think we will decide on that for our first holiday altogether when these dark days are past. Isn't that what you always wanted darling? Getting back to the point, you will be wondering how I came to be under canvas. Well, it was a 24 hour guard 20 miles out of Nottingham. That's the second 24 hr since I came. Have you heard from the Spences at all? If not, you will. For darling the last time I was there they forced my hand by suggesting going to Gatehouse for their holidays which are the last week in May and the first in June.

Darling I had no alternative at the time as I was sitting eating their food but I know you couldn't do with them and it is so near my leave which I pray I will be getting about that time. So darling just leave it to me I will fix it. After all I only had a couple of meals there so I don't feel greatly indebted to them. Darling I suppose the daffodils will be out now. If you could manage it, I would like you to send some to my relation in Edinburgh and chance the address: Miss Cumming, 137 Morrison St, Edinburgh. Put a note in and give her my new address. Now darling if you feel like going to your home by all means go. 3 weeks seems like rather a long time but let me know in good time before you go in case anything should happen. And if I was you, I should find out about what fare the bus would be and if there is little difference by all means go by it as Dumfries is a bad place to get the train. It is just crammed by the time it reaches there. Thinking the whole thing over it seems rather futile after spending all those dreary winter nights at home and I know perfectly well it will not be a rest you will get. However, my darling do whatever you wish. Well dear I am sending your brooch you jealous little thing!! It is the nicest one I could see as I wanted you to have the best sweetheart so hope you will like it. Now I will leave this till I get yours and if there is time add a bit more. Darling yours just to hand today Monday but I seem fated for getting mine sent off, for today I am duty driver. That means I have to stay in the battery office till 10.30 pm tonight and tomorrow there is another scheme but I hope I will get your parcel off sometime tomorrow Tuesday. I am driving a T.L.B truck tomorrow which incidentally is my own. You were naughty to put those matches in as they were not safety ones and I am not kidding when I tell you the fine is £50.

Yes, I will write and thank Capt Short for the cigs. It's funny I always like yours best. I was so thrilled when I saw the tin and when I read who sent them as well, I just wasn't quite so thrilled. No darling these are not private billets just requisitioned houses. Of course, they are not so comfortable and convenient as the barracks. Well darling don't send any eats. I do get enough. I think more than a training Regt unless it looks more in a mess tin!! There is a fish shop close by if I do feel ravenous. I am glad you are keeping better darling. Do let me know how you are after you go to the hospital. Glad Marion and Ann are keeping fit. I expect they are enjoying this spell of nice sunny weather we are having. She must be very sweet and I'm sure good company for you now. Well, my sweetheart I must close now and I will do my best to get this off tomorrow. Bye bye and take great care of yourself. With all my love and kisses to you all. Ever yours Harold Xxxxxx

Joan's brooch

Marion and Ann, aged 3 years and 6 months (left),
and aged 6 and 3 (right)

My Darling

Thanks for yours received yesterday. Well my darling I'm afraid this will have to be short and sweet as I have been so very busy working up to 12.30 at night and do want to get parcel off today and I will write you a longer letter tonight or tomorrow. Yes, I wrote to Capt Short as I thought I had better catch him before he left Cardoness. I wish G. Hunter would hurry and come to Kirkcudbright so as you could get well. Surely he must have been there by now. I always thought he visited once a fortnight. It's time Broadfoot gave you the set potatoes but take it easy when you get them dear. Just do a few lines at a time as it is a very back aching job. Yes, I owe everybody letters. I hope I get time this week to answer some but it is definitely Brenda's turn to write and anyway I did not know her address. Well, my darling I will stop now and get parcel done up ready for the first chance and I will let you have a longer letter by Friday or Saturday. So, bye bye for now. All my love to you all. Ever yours

Harold xxxxxx

My Darling

I expect you have received the parcel alright. I'm afraid it was not a very long letter for last week I had hardly a minute to myself. There was a big draft of 500 came in so I was kept duty driving until the early hours of the morning. They all had to be squeezed into our billets which makes them choc-a- bloc however they will not be here very long as they are going on to the 1st Reserve. Now Darling if you want two letters a week, they will naturally be shorter unless we talk "shop" and I think twice a week of that and you will get bored however we will see. I am writing this in the billet as the majority are on guard and the rest are out so I have a bit of peace and quiet for once. Otherwise, it is hopeless trying to write and the best thing to do is to go down to the H.M Canteen. There is quite a good one in town with a writing room. I have not made any real pals so far. I find it is much more difficult in billets than it was in barracks. We seem more scattered and there is really no-one quite suitable for me in the M.T section with the exception of a L/Bdr who seems to have taken a slight fancy to me so it might mature into closer friendship however I'm not worried. There is one signaller from Redford out of 78 Squad but I only know him by sight. Another signaller I was a bit chummy with and went out once or twice with but we find it difficult to keep in contact with one another as the signallers are in another billet. Of course, I will be able to explain all this better when I see you darling. Now I thought my tests were things of the past but no such perishing luck. Last week I had to have a gruelling test which lasted 4 hours. I ground my teeth and thought I had done quite well and how thankful I was when I switched the engine off on returning then the ground just opened up and the stuffing just dropped out of me when the perisher said, I'm not passing you as I am not quite satisfied

He explained I was very faulty with my driving in traffic but he said as that was the only fault, he would like to give me another test in traffic tomorrow morning. So, with the faults pointed out to me and my better knowledge of Nottingham I do hope I will pass as they only keep 1st class drivers in this unit. I shan't be finishing this till tomorrow so I shall be able to let you know how I get on. Well darling about the cigarette question. I'm afraid I'll have to have yours as you see we are only allowed 30 a week from the Naafi and I'm afraid I smoke double that amount. I know that is scandalous dear but remember sometimes that is the only little comfort I have. However Darling if you find it is too expensive you will just have to cut them down or I could send you the extra money it costs you. As for a drink of beer, that's out of all question. It doesn't worry me. In fact, I wouldn't buy it if I had plenty of money as it is just drinking money now. How do you like the new brown flour for cakes and things? I think they are rather fascinating and they certainly make a change. Darling I have just received your other letter. You may be able to get some before the next parcel. If not just send what you have got. Yes, I received a nice letter from Capt Short. Thank you for sending flowers to Edinburgh dear. I hope it is the right address. Well Darling I passed my ordeal of this morning alright so I hope now I am a full-blown driver. Well, my darling I must close now so take great care of yourself. All my love and kisses to you all.

Ever yours
Harold
xxxxx

P.S I have not had time to write to the Spences yet but if you should hear in the meantime don't answer it but let me know what she says.

RANKS

Gunner (Gnr) is a rank equivalent to private in the British Army Royal Artillery.

Driver (Dvr) is a military rank in the British Army. It is also equivalent to the rank of private.

The next highest rank is usually lance bombardier.

26/GS Publications/938

INSPECTION, MAINTENANCE AND CARE
of
ARMY VEHICLES
(Wheeled)

BASED ON THE " TASK " SYSTEM

(This pamphlet supersedes the 1942 Edition.)

*Prepared under the direction of
The Chief of the Imperial General Staff*

THE WAR OFFICE,
July, 1943.

This pamphlet must be carried in the pocket by all officers and NCOs IC Vehicles and Motor Cycles.

... like I did at Edinburgh and I did not make one mistake so everything in the garden was lovely. It takes 5 days to pass out here so next week I shall be right in the thick of it but I feel very confident the I.C. part is really simpler here than it was at Edinburgh. There is just the winching and driving the big armoured cars that drag the guns that I am doubtful about but I'll manage it and the other things we have to do will be child's play to me as I got a first class grounding at Edinburgh. I had a letter from my learned friend in Edinburgh. He tells me he failed and has been relegated so that means another six weeks of that blessed buzzer for him. The 79 Squad is completely broken up. Some are in England and about 7 picked ones are awaiting embarkation, two are NCOs at Redford so that's that. I see in the Galloway News that Jardine the plumber's daughter had a very fine wedding. Yes, there is a lad a few beds away from mine by the name of Murray. He says he is a very far distant relation to the Gatehouse ones. He lives at Kirkcudbright. He has the Galloway News sent him every week so I get a look at it. Well darling I won't write any more just now and see if your parcel comes. If it doesn't come by Monday, I will send this off.

Darling your parcel came this morning. I am so pleased and it just saved my life as I was *[Incomplete]*

Nottingham

Sunday

My Darling

I am starting this today as I won't get any time tomorrow as I have got to drive an officer somewhere which is going to take all day as I have to draw rations in the morning. In any case I must have your letter written soon for as soon as the parcel arrives, I have to get cracking to get it off again and take the first chance of catching a post. The American cloth idea might be alright but what I should be afraid of would be it getting too conspicuous. Once a thing gets marked the next step is to find out what's in it. The bad point here is that half the G.P.O. is controlled by the military and they put it down as the reason things go missing. I must touch wood! I had thought of a cardboard box which could be treated in the same manner by sticking labels on but maybe you would find it difficult to get one of those now. I will see if I can get some brown paper in the town sometime and start by sticking labels on it. Well, my darling I think it is a pity Mrs Boyes and family are not coming as I think she would have been a bit more company for you, however if they find they cannot get the daily person they might change their mind. Thank you for sending flowers to Edinburgh. I hope I have got the right number and if so, we should get a reply. Now my dear they keep you hellish busy here. I hope I shall be able to keep up with it. Darling I think I am getting a bit of my flesh back as the food is a bit more substantial here and I can get a few good feeds in the town so I am stuffing as much as I can. I heard from Brenda today and she said she sent me 60 cigs which have gone with the wind. I have an idea Doris must have written too unless she isn't well or something. Well darling I will close now. With all my love to you all and heaps and heaps to you alone darling.

Ever yours Harold
Xxxxx

Darling this is Tuesday and still no parcel so I have the wind up a bit. I hope it hasn't got lost or that anything is wrong at home. However, if I don't receive it tomorrow, I will send this letter on.

Bye bye dear

Well darling I have just received your letter so that means my parcel has disappeared. I am very cut up about it. The only thing is you will have to register them. Will you send me a towel that one I had before will do. That will save me having to pay for that. I will just have the shirt and socks to pay for. Let me know what else was in it. I don't know what I shall do about pants as it rather cold to wear the thin ones yet.

My darling

I am just about recovering from the shock and disappointment of losing my parcel. I only wish I could lay hands on the dirty hounds that took it. It's funny, I had the feeling I should lose one however darling you will have to register them now. The postman will do it and bring you the receipt in the morning. You will have to seal the knots so don't make any more than you can help. I have bought a piece of sealing wax for you so will enclose it. Darling I was hoping you would send the towel on right away but I hope it arrives tomorrow as the one I have is so very dirty. It's going to be awkward with the shirts only having two but will just have to manage the best way we can until there is another kit check then I shall have to pay for it and I will see if I can get another one then. I will put on a pair of the other pants so as I can get the parcel off tomorrow, Monday. I heard from your Ma so everything is alright there. Also had a line from Brenda. She says she sent 60 cigs but I never received them. I don't know what's wrong with Doris as I haven't heard from her for weeks. Well, my darling I must finish this now and get your parcel done up so hope you and my little girls are quite well.

All my love and kisses to you sweetheart.
Ever yours
Harold
Xxxxx

Marion said Ardwell House was burnt. Does that mean
it was burnt down?

I thought Mrs Floss would end up that way. I suppose that will be another upset. Haven't all the land girls arrived yet?

My Darling

Thanks for your letter and parcel which I did receive this time but you must register them in future for that was such a big loss and I am afraid there is nothing I can do about it for that is the first thing they say, was it registered? And of course, with it being such a big haul with all those cigs in. My future parcels will certainly be marked and it wouldn't be long before another went but if they are registered, I should stand a better chance of getting them all safe. I'm afraid they would take the sugar out of your tea if you didn't keep a damn good watch on it. I heard from Doris darling and she says she sent me some cigs which I have never seen but that is a little more plausible as she evidently sent them to Bonhill. All the same I have been unfortunate with my smokes. Now darling I hope you are feeling all right as you have not had anything done for your little complaint yet and I hope it is none the worse for your great gardening effort. I think you have done well if they grow the right way up!!! Don't touch them now till I come home. I don't think they will be tall enough to hoe until that time. I hope you put my gardening tools back alright. You did not tell me the contents of my cousin's letter dear. Did she say she might be writing to me? Evidently the address was alright. Yes darling, maybe you're right. I shouldn't have spun such yarns to the Spences. Maybe that's why I lost my parcel, however it cannot be altered now and just to give my leave as an excuse wouldn't have been sufficient for people think you should make sacrifices. It's funny neither of us has heard from them yet but I am not worried. Fancy Ardwell being burnt down.

Maybe it was to get it out of the way. When does Mrs Jennings event come off? He must have changed his mind about other people's families being sufficient for Louise to play with. Well Darling I thought it about time I wrote a line to Dorothy especially as I was no great distance away from her home, with the result I heard from her this morning and she is coming to see me on Saturday so I hope I shall be free to go out. Isn't that nice of her? What a sudden change in the weather. It is quite hot here now. I think the parcel after this next one had better contain my thin vest and I want you to keep the thick ones safe at home and I will let you know if I want you to send them back in a hurry. Now my darling I must catch the post so take great care of yourself. With all my love to you all. Ever yours Harold

M.xxx
A.xxx
You my pet xxxxx

Harold and Marion Cardoness Bay

*Marion and Ann, aged 6 and 3 years (left),
and aged 8 and 5 years (right)*

My dear Marion

Thank you for your last letter. It is awful about Ardwell isn't it? Did you see it burning? I hope no one got burnt. I saw Aunty Dorothy yesterday and I was telling her what a big girl you were now. I think she wants to come and spend a holiday with Mummy this summer so you will be seeing her. I am not sure if I can put any chocs in the parcel this week as I want to send some to Granny but I know you won't mind for once. Now I hope you are being a good girl and helping mummy. Bye bye for now with lots of love from Daddy to you and Ann.

Xxxx
P.T.O
I have just got mummy's letter saying you have a sore knee. I hope by now it is nearly better.
Daddy

My Darling

I thought I might have got your parcel yesterday but I don't expect you could manage to get the washing done by that time. Anyway, I will look out for it tomorrow. I think they take a bit longer when they are registered. Well darling I saw Dorothy yesterday. There is certainly a transformation. She is quite drawn and haggard looking. She has had all her top teeth out which doesn't improve matters. I felt quite sorry for her but my opinion is unchanged in fact more concrete than it was before for I could see beyond that deep sorrow and her selfishness will not be improved by her great loss. All this is just between ourselves darling so don't repeat it to the family. Her mother sent a message inviting me for a weekend but I explained to her about not getting weekends. She had to leave by the 5.30 pm bus and I was not sorry as it was the work of art trying to keep the subject off poor Jim. I heard from Doris and she says she sent me some cigs but she sent them to Bonhill so may never have left there. She says Dick may be called up next month but I expect you will have heard all this. I also heard from Brenda. She was informing me it was her birthday and saying she was getting 48 hours and going home. How she can do it beats me. I didn't send her anything. For one thing I have no money and the other her brooch was to be considered as a birthday present. Bath and Norwich had an awful doing last week. Many streets in Bath are now level to the ground. Now my darling I will put in for my leave for the first week in June. I have not quite made my mind up which date but it would be either the 3rd or the 5th. Does this suit you darling, you know in every way?

I could leave it till later but you must let me know this week as I have to get my application through which takes about a fortnight. Darling I am longing to be home again and I do hope things will go right this time. It is so awfully disappointing when they don't. It has turned devilish cold again. Good job there is no spuds up or the frost would have got them. Well sweetheart I will leave this till tomorrow and see if yours comes.

My Darling thanks for the parcel. I got the wind up again as I have only just received it and it appears I should not have the billet address put on so in the future dear alter the address to c/o G.P.O Nottingham, especially the registered ones. Now darling you don't sound very cheerful maybe because you are not feeling very well. I do hope your throat will soon be better. I don't think you are taking great care of yourself as much as you should. I am sorry to hear of wee Marion's knee. I do hope you will be able to get it better and nothing complicating sets in. The knee is such a funny place. Now darling about the crockery. I'm afraid it will be hopeless as there doesn't seem to be any about here either. In the restaurants and eating places you have to put up with cups without handles and pieces out. If I am not on duty on Saturday, I will take a look round the market and see if there is anything round there. Now darling I will close and get this off today (Tuesday). Darling the string was half off the parcel but everything was alright.

Bye bye dear.
Hope you are feeling better.
All my love to you all.
Ever your
Harold
Xxxxxx

My Darling

I have just received your letter on coming in at 6.15 pm and it worries me very much. It is all very disappointing and disheartening. Of course, that is what we are fighting for or maybe we shall see when it is over for, I'm afraid it will have to be different this time to what it was after the last war. Well, my darling I cannot decide anything at the moment as I will have to think it over but there is one thing certain you are not going to work unless there is a great improvement in your health and I certainly couldn't go on with such uneasiness of mind for every day I look for a letter saying you have got to clear out or something. If only you could get a convenient little place where you could pay rent. It would ease our minds all round. I'm afraid the car will have to go my dear for it is going to be a millstone round our necks. If only you could have driven, it might have made a difference. I will put in for leave for the 3rd June. Well darling I do hope you will be all right on Friday. I shall be thinking of you and wondering how you are so let me know soon. I do hope it is nothing very serious. I hope you got the parcel alright. No, I haven't heard from my cousin or my aunt in Slough or Harold and Hilda. If you are writing to them you might give them my address as I have no money for stamps just now. I heard from Allan Tait (my learned friend) this morning. He is now at West Wickham and just got back from his embarkation leave so evidently his wangling was all in vain. Well, my darling I must close now and get this posted now. Don't worry too much for something will turn up in the end surely or this rotten world is not worth living in. Take great care of yourself and the children. All my love to you all

Ever your
Harold
Xxxxxx

243/61 A/Tk Regt R.A.
Lille Barracks
Aldershot

Friday

My Darling

Just a little line letting you know where I have landed. Don't send parcel yet I will drop you a line on Monday and if I want it send it right away registered. I got into awful bother not having all my kit so I will probably have to send the army stuff to the laundry. I managed to get a filthy old pair of socks and I got a second hand shirt to replace those I lost so that saved me 10/-. Well, my darling I hope you got over your little ordeal all right and you are feeling well. Now darling I must close and catch a post of some sort. All my love to you all.

Ever yours Harold Xxxxx

My Darling

I expect you got my wire and letter alright and my parcel will be on the way. I will not receive it anyway until Thursday night as I am off on a 3 day scheme. I was all ready to come on leave today even had my pass and ration card when I was stopped to go on this scheme. This has been a nasty blow darling but I will explain everything when I see you. I will be home either Friday night or Saturday morning, so unless you hear from me again expect me on Saturday morning as I expect I will be travelling by night train. I hoped to get your letter saying how you are. I do hope you are alright. Do take care of yourself sweetheart. It is very hot down here so I am hoping you have put a thin vest in as well. When I come back from leave, I will have to send the army stuff to the laundry as I got an awful row for sending it home. Of course, they said it was risking W.D property in the post. Well, my own darling I will close now so hope this finds you and my little girls quite well. Bye bye till Saturday.

All my love.
Ever yours

Harold

xxxxx

It wouldn't matter about not putting the troop on the parcel. I wasn't in a troop when I was writing the letter.

L Troop
254/61 AMK Regt R.A
Lille Barracks
Aldershot

My darling little wife

Just a hurried line letting you know I arrived back safely and I hope you done the same. I arrived at St Pancreas at 9.30 am. I arrived at my aunt's door exactly on the stroke of 12 so I thought of you opening our door at exactly the same time if you caught the 10 bus. I hope everything went all right with you darling and you got something to eat before leaving. I am glad I had my aunts to go to as I don't think I could have faced coming straight back here. They were quite nice to me. They have a really nice flat in the most charming surroundings I have ever seen. It was so unique being so close to the town. My cousin John has not altered very much apart from his "tach" which made him look funny in the snaps. I think he will marry this year. She looks like a very nice girl by her snaps. She is in the WAAFs now. I think my aunt and cousin will make an attempt to see you in July. I got back to billets by 10pm and got busy with my kit and bed and finally managed to get between the blankets by 11 and believe me I didn't want much rocking, although I did manage to get about 4 hrs sleep on the train. I woke just as we were coming into Derby. I have not seen Lakes since my return. I think he must have been shifted to another battery but when

I get the time, I will have a hunt for him. It has been a busy day today. We have only just finished at 7.30 pm so I doubt if I will catch a post tonight. I am hoping there will be a late one. I was before the M.O this morning also the Major and thinking of you and the kiddies I done my utmost. I hate to dishearten you my darling but I am afraid it was all in vain, however we can still live in hopes. I think we will be here all this week so try and get a letter back to me. This afternoon we were inspected by the King and Queen.

It will probably be in tomorrow's papers so if you happen to see one have a look. Now my darling for my sake and your own be very brave and do your best for the children and the home and above all take great care of yourself then when the time comes for me to come home how wonderful it will be and you really will have been fighting by my side. I hope it will turn out that you will be able to stay in the wee lodge but if not, I hope you will be able to decide on something that will be a help but is not too hard and will keep you happy.

Do let me know what is happening darling. Now I must close and get this posted so bye bye sweetheart. Keep your chin up. All my love to you all.

Ever yours
Harold
Xxxxxx
P.S I hope Marion was alright when you got back.

My darling

I have wangled these vests so please keep them at home for me. Would you wash these socks and towel and send them back as soon as you possibly can? Have been on commando training hence the socks. Hope you are well. All my love

Yours ever
Harold

Harold on his motorbike, 1920s

Harold carried this photo of Joan and Marion in his wallet during the North Africa campaign

The Old Lodge, 2017

Joan's brother Jim in his navy uniform and Dorothy

Hearty Greetings

The pleasant path of memory,
Has led direct to you.
With hearty wishes for Christmas,
And for the New Year too.

Wishing you every happiness
at Christmas and throughout
the Coming Year

from: Harold with Love and
best wishes to you all.

A Christmas card sent from North Africa

*A camel bracelet brought back from
Africa for Marion*

*1939–1945 Star, Africa Star, Italy Star,
War Medal 1939–1945*

My Darling

I find I came away without my leather belt after all, it will still be on the old grey flannels. If this reaches you in time will you put it in with the towel and socks. I hope I get them back in time. It is awful not having the slightest idea where we will move. It is so terribly hot my face is almost a cinder. If only it had been like this when I was on leave. I have seen Lakes. He is now in HQ so I see very little of him. The Jewish fellow is also being moved so I shall be left in the room by myself. I will probably see if there is room somewhere else as it will not be good for me to stay by myself although I much prefer it. Darling I am longing to hear from you. It is a week tomorrow since I left and I have not heard from you. I know it is not your fault sweetheart. I don't know what I shall do when I have to wait weeks. I enjoy the tobacco you bought me very much darling. I usually have a pipe on going to bed then I can sit and think at the same time. Well, my darling I must finish this and catch the post. There is not time for anything when we are finished here so bye bye for now all my love to you and lots of big hugs and kisses to you all.

Take great care of yourselves
Ever yours
Harold
Xxxxxxx

Harold, Marion and Ann

My own darling

Thanks for your nice letter but up to now I haven't received parcel. I am so glad you got on alright at Dumfries and arrived back home safely and I hope Marion was not too disappointed when she learned what had happened. Yes darling, I quite understand how you are placed and whatever you do don't shift the furniture out of the lodge until you are quite settled on a place to move to and do not weaken at the last moment and take it to your home against your will. If you can't find a suitable place in the time they give you just stay put until you get somewhere for they can't put you on the street and there is bags of room in that big house for married couples or farm hands. Darling I think you would be wise to keep a look out while you are working there, just in case. You can always turn anything down if you see you are going to be kept on there. Whatever happens I do hope you will be alright. It will be better if you have some little thing extra to do as it will help pass the days quicker. It is a terrific waste of our lives sweetheart but I am hoping one day we will make up for it in full. Darling I don't want you to suffer. I'll do any of that, I want you to be as happy as you possibly can. Make yourself happy with the children my dear don't worry about me. Just take great care of yourself and the children and our little home then we shall be all ready to start where we left off when I come back. I have not written to anyone else yet, I have just not felt in the mood but I must do so soon as we have been warned not to write or send telegrams on the day we leave. Of course, I will do my best to let you know somehow but if you don't hear you will quite understand. I expect you received my parcel with awful socks in. Now I am puzzled what to do as I am left with a dirty shirt and another pair of socks and I don't think I dare risk them. We had to go through Commando Training that day.

We had to go through barbed wire and water up to our waist and mud and slime up above our knees and just to make things more pleasant, bombs and things exploding all around us. All this in full battle order including rifle. I thought I was going to drop at the end of it, however I have got over it alright but I am not looking forward to any more. The Major is very understanding about the ages of men. He was very glad to see me still standing at the finish but the Col doesn't care a damn. He just greeted us with the words "Well done lads but that is only an atom to what you have to go through yet" so the Lord help us. I had a letter from Brenda. Just the usual tripe. In fact, the exact replica of yours as of course she did not know I was on leave. I also got one from Dorothy which had been forwarded from Nottingham so it must have arrived just after I left. There's something I don't like about Dorothy. I think Doris will be right in the end. Oh, I don't think I told you, my aunt sent cigs to Bonhill also so that's another one I did not receive. Yes, my aunt and cousin said they might probably come to see you for a few days at the end of the month but I expect they will let you know. I am supposed to go and see them again but I can't see how it can be done from this hole as we are never finished. There is no specific time off whatsoever and this terrible suspense hangs over one like the gallows so really, I am just living from day to day. I have wondered if Percy Boyes is round this way as there are some R.H.C near here. If you are writing to her give her my address then if he should be here, he might try and find me. It is all so hopeless to me just now. I have not heard from my learned friend so perhaps he is away. Well my darling I must close once more or I shall never get the other letters written which I must do in "case" they are the last for a while. I am hoping your wonderful faith will prove its worth my dear.

Keep smiling sweetheart. All my love to you all. Ever yours Harold
Xxxxx

P.S. Oh darling I just thought of this code just in "case". I will number one of the pages. We will have to be careful as some have been caught coding and have been severely punished and we have been warned. I hardly think they would rumble one little figure on the top of a page! Well, here it is. I will mark the second page.

2 = Libya
2/ = Egypt (probably Cairo)
II = Jerusalem
If I mark the third page also
3 = India (probably Bombay)

That's all I can think of dear, so hope you will make it out. Oh, my learned friend has not been away. He was at the castle on Friday being X-rayed but no sign of his ticket yet. He has to report sick here again. He may be regraded but I doubt if he will get his ticket.

I'm afraid something has gone wrong with my pyjama jacket darling. I hope you will be able to fix it.

Cheerio.

Xx

I have written to Mrs McMath thanking her for scones and told her I am likely to be shifted any day. That will stop her sending any more just now. Apart from that darling don't say anymore to anyone.

My Darling

I have not received the package you said you had sent so if you registered it make a claim for it. I hope you got my other parcels alright and the socks and towel are on the way back as I am expecting to go any day now. I feel sure it will be this week. I hope you are getting on alright Darling and wee Ann's bites are better. It is a lot cooler here today. I wondered if you would remember my other thin vest but it doesn't matter if you didn't as I will manage. Don't chance sending the other pants back. I will be alright with the army two. I wish you had not been so far away so I could have seen you again. However, take great care of yourself and let's hope the time will go very quickly. So, bye bye sweetheart. Keep smiling and don't forget to make enquiries about your parcel. All my love to you all.

Ever yours Harold Xxxxxx

POST  OFFICE

TELEGRAM

Prefix.	Time handed in.	Office of Origin and Service Instructions.	Word
20			

No. _____

STAMP

14 MAY 42

4

From _____ 120 5/59 NOTTINGHAM 11   To _____

BISHOP OLD LODGE CARDONESS: GATEHOUSEOFFLEET

CASTLEDOUGLAS =

LEAVING HERE TOMORROW FRIDAY = HAROLD + +

Monday 4 pm

My Own Darling

Just a few hurried lines giving you an address which I think will find me but I am not too sure. If I get anything more definite, I will try and get it through but chance this for the time being. It will be censored of course so use your discretion. Now Darling the hour has almost arrived. We leave tonight, Monday 15th. I am feeling it very much but I must not weaken. I must be brave. I think that will be the best attitude to take for us all. Thank you for your two letters I received this morning. The post had come and most chaps had got their last minute letters but none appeared for me so I was feeling rather sick at heart but to my great joy yours and one from Doris turned up about a couple of hours after. They must have got overlooked somewhere. I see one of yours was dated the 9th so it must have been dancing around some place but I was so glad to get them. Please tell Doris I received her cigs and letter and thank her very much. I will write to her when I can but it may be some weeks. Now don't worry darling if you don't hear from me for several weeks. No news will be good news. For any news on the wireless or in the papers it will be under the heading of "Highland Division" I expect. I shall be driving an R.L (reconnaissance) truck when we reach the other side. There is a huge map of this Island in this canteen and nearly every day I take a look at the little bay and picture you picnicking there and the wee ones paddling. I will take one last and longing look as I go out now. Sweetheart be very brave and happy for my sake. Take the greatest care of yourself for me. I shall no doubt have to come through Hell but what matters so long as I have your dear sweet self to meet at the end.

Darling who knows, it may be a lot sooner than we think but whatever the length of time my precious I shall always be waiting and longing for you. Do think of me in that way darling. Darling we must both live for the day when we shall be together again and let us think that day is not such a great distance off and don't worry sweetheart. Keep cheerful and happy because I want to see you exactly your same dear self when I return. Thank wee Marion for her nice letter. I am pleased she is getting on so well at school. Give her a big kiss from me, also wee Ann. Hope you got my other letter also. I sent a bit more choc to Marion. I expect she will share it between you all. Now goodbye my dearest. All my love and do keep your chin up. Bye bye. God bless you. Ever yours Harold Xxxxxx

P.S. If you go home for a holiday you had better leave your address at the P.O. in case anything should come for you
Goodbye sweetheart Xx

My dear Marion

Daddy is going away for a long time so that means I will not see you quite so often. I may be going where all the little black girls and boys live but I will have to tell you all about them when I come home again. Now I want you to be a good girl and help Mummie then she will be very happy. Be a good girl at school and try hard with your lessons and learn as much as you can for when you are a very big girl you will be glad you did. Take care of your little sister and I hope you will have some nice times together. Mummie will no doubt take you down for some bathes if she has time so don't forget your swimming lessons also your P.Ts. It will not be very long before Ann is starting school too. That will be nice for you. Don't forget to help Mummie with the potatoes just like you used to for me.

Bye bye for now with a big hug and kiss from Daddy to you both.
Ever your loving Daddy
xx xx

EMBARKATION 1942

Date	Location	
16 · 6 · 42	Liverpool	
20 · 6 · 42	Gourack	
8 · 7 · 42	FreeTown	Africa
18 · 7 · 42	Cape Town	"
6 · 8 · 42	Aden	
13 · 8 · 42	Port Tewfic	Egypt
14 · 8 · 42	Cairo	"
23 · 10 · 42	Alamein	"
25 · 12 · 42	EL Aghiela	"
27 · 1 · 43	Tripoli	"
21 · 2 · 43	Gabes	
22 · 2 · 43	Souse	
10 · 4 · 43	Sfax	
13 · 5 · 43	Bougie	N. Africa
6 · 8 · 43	Sicily	
9 · 10 · 43	97 General Hospital. N.A.	

Harold's log of his travels

L. Troop
243/61 A/tk Regt R.A.
c/o A.P.O 2005.

My Darling
Just a last minute good
bye and to let you know
address to reply as I didn't
put it quite right before.
I am on the boat and quite
comfortable and well. Take
great care of yourself the
children and everything may
soon be back until then
all the best along with all
my love
Ever Yours
Harold

XXXXXX

MY DARLING

Hope you are all well. I have sent three letters so hope you get them. You might receive them about the time of your birthday so here's wishing you Many Happy Returns. I hope I shall be home for your next one.

Longing for a letter from you.
All my love and kisses
Ever Yours
Harold
Xxxx

1130250 Dvr. Bishop H
L Troop
243/61 A/Tk Regt. R.A
c/o A.P.O 2005

My darling

Just a few lines letting you know I am safe and well except for feeling like a grease spot. In fact as I write this the water is streaming down me like a drain pipe and all I am wearing is a pair of shorts and I suppose this is mild compared to what we will get. I shall be glad to hear from you darling as I am wondering how you are getting on. Goodness knows when that will be as I have no idea when or where we shall land. I had hoped to get one from you before we left our dear old shores but I didn't so must just wait patiently. Has my aunt from Slough been to see you yet? Perhaps dear you would drop her a line telling her I am away and explain how it was I didn't get to see her again, also I would be glad if you wrote and told my cousin in Edinburgh and give her this address if you like. I am getting plenty of cigs on the boat and at cost price. They have cut our pay down and we just get it once a fortnight but it is plenty with the cigs and beer being so cheap. I am not allowed to tell you the name of this boat however I hope to be able to show you it in my shipping books when I come home again. How are my little girls? I expect Marion has started her summer holidays. Are you going home? If you are, I hope you all have a nice time and give my love to everyone. If I get time, I will write to Doris today. Well, my darling I hope you are well and happy. Let me know exactly how you all are and how things are going on and may the time pass very quickly to the time I shall be coming home again. All my love to you all and take great care of yourselves.

Ever yours
Harold Xxxxxx

P.S. I was just thinking if poor old Jim hadn't gone on that blessed minesweeper he may have been on the escort for this convoy, that would have been great.

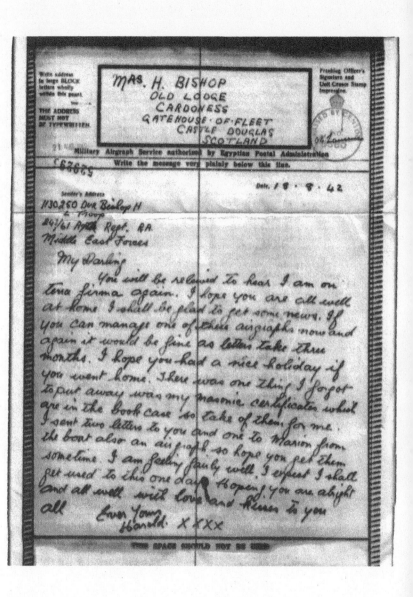

MRS. H. BISHOP
OLD LODGE
CARDONESS
GATEHOUSE · OF · FLEET
CASTLE DOUGLAS
SCOTLAND

Military Airgraph Service authorised by Egyptian Postal Administration

Write the message very plainly below this line.

Date. 18 · 8 · 42

Sender's Address
1130250 Dvr Bishop H
& Tharp
84/61 Ryth Regt. RA
Middle East Forces

My Darling

You will be relieved to hear I am on terra firma again. I hope you are all well at home I shall be glad to get some news. If you can manage one of these airgraphs now and again it would be fine as letters take three months. I hope you had a nice holiday if you went home. There was one thing I forgot to put away was my masonic certificates which are in the book case so take of them for me. I sent two letters to you and one to Marion from the boat also an airgraph so hope you get them sometime. I am feeling fairly well, I expect I shall get used to this one day hoping you are alright and all well with love and kisses to you all

Ever Yours
Harold. X XXX

MRS H. BISHOP
CARDONESS
GATEHOUSE · OF · FLEET
CASTLE DOUGLAS
SCOTLAND

Military Airgraph Service authorized by Egyptian Postal Administration

Write the message very plainly below this line.

Sender's Address 1130250 Dvr Bishop H
L Troop
242/6 A/Tk Regt. R.A.
Middle East Forces

Date. 4 · 9 · 42

My Darling
    This is the 2 airgraph I have sent from
here as I have not heard from you yet and I
am wondering if everything is all right for you.
I hope you have received all my other correspondence
alright. Will you send me an air mail post card it
will cost 1/d and will reach me in about a fortnight
lots of the lads seem to be getting them. Well my
darling I am getting used to the heat of the desert
now and so far have kept fairly well. I celebrated
my birthday with another regt which I was attached
to for a few days and really had a nice day as
we went to a salt water lake where I had my
first bathe it was lovely and warm. I hope you
have had a nice summer and plenty of bathing
and I hope you are all well and happy. Now
do try and let me have some news soon
all my love to you all
                    Ever yours
                        Harold XXXXX

THIS SPACE SHOULD NOT BE USED

120

DEPLOYMENT

The 51st (H) Division A/T Regiment sailed for Egypt on 16th June 1942, landing on 12th August after completing their training in Scotland.

CITY OF CAPE TOWN

INFORMATION

for

VISITING TROOPS

(SOLDIERS, SAILORS, AIRMEN)

With particulars of Free Entertainments, Refreshments, etc.

General information may be obtained at the

VISITORS' INFORMATION BUREAU

LOWER ADDERLEY STREET
No. 1 on Map
(Left-hand side going up, below Railway Station)

TELEPHONE 2-5714

and also at the

NATIONAL COUNCIL OF WOMEN'S INFORMATION KIOSK, DOCK ROAD

Telephone 2-0766

The following facilities are at the disposal of Visiting Troops.

REFRESHMENT CANTEENS, REST ROOMS, ETC.—The principal central canteen and rest room is behind the City Hall in Darling Street, in the MAYOR'S GARDEN, marked A on the Map. Open daily : refreshments are provided and there are rest rooms, reading and writing facilities, games and dancing every evening.

GOOD CHEER CLUB.—4th Floor, Garlick's Building, Adderley Street (E on Map). Refreshments, games, dancing in evening. Open at 5.30 p.m. when troop convoys are in port, otherwise on Tuesday, Wednesday and Saturday evenings only.

YOUNG MEN'S CHRISTIAN ASSOCIATION.—44 Long Street (corner of Hout Street, B on Map). Reading and writing facilities, meals and refreshments at reduced charges ; telephone 2-2959.

MISSION TO SEAMEN'S INSTITUTE, Alfred Street (on right above Dock Gates). Open daily ; refreshment canteen, reading and writing facilities, entertainments, dances and films ; free teas and tram tickets.

ST. ANDREW'S HALL (Presbyterian Church).—Somerset Road (R on Map). Refreshments, games, letter-writing, etc. Entertainments are also organised and arrangements made for outings.

SALVATION ARMY : REST ROOM.—Loop Street (C on Map). Refreshments, recreation, writing facilities, etc. Open daily except Saturday and Sunday.

METROPOLITAN HALL (Methodist Church).—Corner of Burg and Church Streets (D on Map). Refreshments, rest rooms, writing facilities. Open every second Saturday and Sunday. Evening entertainments.

FAIRHAVEN WORK PARTY ROOMS, 40 Darling Street (G on Map). Refreshments ; arrangements made for outings.

CATHEDRAL HALL.—Queen Victoria Street (F on Map). Used as an "overflow" canteen as required.

SOLDIERS CLUB.—Church Square (M on Map). Sleeping accommodation and meals at nominal charges ; hot and cold showers. Recreations, games, billiards, etc.

UNION JACK CLUB.—Top of Plein Street (behind St. Mary's Cathedral, J on Map). Troops with shore leave may obtain accommodation for the night at the Club. Grill room, billiards, etc. Hot and cold baths.

CATHOLIC CLUB FOR SERVICE MEN.—11 Hope Street (on left opposite St. Mary's Cathedral, K on Map). Refreshments, rest and writing rooms. Open Saturdays : 3 to 7 p.m. ; Sundays : 11 a.m. to 1 p.m., and every afternoon when troop convoys are in port.

DEMOCRATIC WOMEN'S LEAGUE REST ROOM.—Pragtus Lane (L on Map). Open 10 a.m. to 11 p.m. ; Sundays : 6 p.m. to 11 p.m. Meals at nominal charges ; refreshments, games, dancing and music.

TATTERSALLS TEA ROOMS.—Aldabroza Buildings, 58 Loop Street, corner Castle Street (above R on Map). Open Weekdays 10 a.m. to 7 p.m. and Sundays when troop convoys are in port. Recreation, games, etc. Meals at reduced prices.

ZIONIST HALL CANTEEN (Union of Jewish Women).—14 Hope Street (right side, O on Map). Open when troopships in port, 2 p.m. to 11.30 p.m., except Fridays and Saturdays, before 8 p.m. Meals and refreshments, games, dancing, outings arranged.

TOC H REST ROOM.—Fletcher's Chambers, 15 Adderley Street. Open from 5 to 10 p.m. when troopships are in. Refreshments.

TOC H ELLISON HOUSE SERVICE WOMEN'S CLUB.—Old Post Office, Adderley Street. Sleeping accommodation, lounges, dining room.

OUTSIDE THE CITY.

RONDEBOSCH RENTAL CLUB.—Main Road, Rondebosch. Open daily. Refreshments, recreation, etc. Dancing in evening. Outings arranged.

CAMPS BAY—C.P.S. CANTEEN.—Open 2 to 10.30 p.m. when troop convoys are in port and week-ends 5 to 10 p.m. Refreshments, games, music. Take A1 bus outside Visitors' Bureau, Adderley Street.

SIMONSTOWN.—NAVAL RECREATION HALL, East Dockyard. Open daily for light refreshments, reading, writing and games. Dances are also arranged. RECREATION HALL, Main Street. Open daily. Light refreshments, games, reading and writing. Concerts and dances arranged.

TRANSPORT.

EXCURSIONS to beauty spots and places of interest are arranged by the Women's Auxiliary Services. Enquiries regarding these trips can also be made at the S.A.W.A.S. Office, Goodwin's Building, Dock Road.

ENTERTAINMENTS.

DANCING at Mayor's Garden Canteen, Rondebosch Service Club, Good Cheer Club, Simonstown Recreation Halls, Democratic Women's Rooms, Zionist Hall Canteen, and in Suburban Municipal Halls.

CINEMAS.—Film shows at all the principal cinema theatres are open to visiting soldiers and sailors at reduced prices.

ORCHESTRA CONCERTS.—Troops are admitted free to all concerts of the Cape Town Municipal Orchestra on Thursday and Sunday evenings in the City Hall, Darling Street (No. 10 on Map).

CHURCH SERVICES.

You are cordially invited to attend services at city and suburban churches. The following are indicated on the Map :—St. George's Cathedral (Anglican), No. 23 ; St. Andrew's (Presbyterian), No. 1 ; Metrodist, next to D ; Baptist, No. 28 ; St. Mary's Cathedral (Roman Catholic), No. 14 ; Congregational, No. 29 ; St. Barnabas (Anglican), No. 30 ; Christian Science, No. 31 ; Presbyterian, No. 32 ; Synagogue, No. 33 ; Salvation Army, C.

SPORT.

GOLF, TENNIS, BOWLS and other games can be arranged for troops ; also matches between naval or military teams. **HORSE RACING** at Kenilworth or Milnerton courses on Saturdays is also free. Enquire at Kiosk or Information Bureau for details. Troops are invited also to watch the Football or Cricket Matches held on Saturday afternoons at Newlands (Football season April to October, Cricket October to March). Take Tram No. 12 or electric train, from Adderley Street.

SWIMMING AND BATHING.

ALL MUNICIPAL BATHING POOLS AND PAVILIONS are free to visiting soldiers and sailors, and costumes and towels are loaned free of charge. The nearest to the Long Street Baths (No. 19 on Map) ; also Camps Bay warm-baths ; take bus A1 from Adderley Street ; and Woodstock warm-baths. Enquire at Visitors' Bureau for directions.

The following organisations are anxious to assist in the entertainment of visiting troops, who are cordially invited to make contact :

ROTARY CLUB. Rotarian hospitality can be arranged through the Information Kiosk, Dock Road.

MASONIC FELLOWSHIP. Visiting Brethren are cordially invited to telephone any of the following : J. Russell (5-6661 or 5-1830) ; A. A. Wincsor (5-8906 or 4-4061) ; T. Nimmo (2-9294 or 4-6111).

TOC H. Members or friends are invited to get in touch ; telephone 2-9294.

THE WOMEN'S CHRISTIAN TEMPERANCE UNION welcomes visitors in the mornings at 144 Longmarket Street.

OVERSEAS LEAGUE. Headquarters, Settlers' Club, 60 Queen Victoria Street, B.C.S. Telephone : 7-2773.

E.A.O.B. (Stuerled' Lodge). Meetings every Tuesday evening at 8 p.m. at Alhbama Hotel, Roeko Street (off Long Street). Take trams Nos. 4 or 6 from St. George's Street, Secretary. Telephone 2-9746.

UNION OF JEWISH WOMEN : 506 (5th floor), Alhame House, 48 St. George's Street, Telephone 2-1673. If any society or organisation you are interested in is not in above list (e.g. Boy Scouts, M.R.A., M.O.T.H., etc.) please ask at the Information Bureau which has a list of local addresses.

SOME HINTS AND SUGGESTIONS.

Cape Town is anxious to make your stay as pleasant as possible ; please do not be afraid to ask your hosts if there is anything you specially want to see or do.

MEALS AND REFRESHMENTS. You will be cordially welcomed at any of the canteens and organisations mentioned.

EXCURSIONS. There are many famous beauty-spots around Cape Town and excursions are well worth while. There are beautiful places to visit along the False Bay coast ; take electric train (from Station, No. 2 on Map) to Muizenberg, or No. 12 bus from Adderley Street as far as Wynberg and train for remainder of the way. The run to Camps Bay by bus (A1 from outside Visitors' Bureau in Adderley Street) is another pleasant one ; also ask about Kirstenbosch Gardens, Rhodes Memorial Zoo, Constantia.

EVENING ENTERTAINMENTS. You are assured of a pleasant social evening at the Canteens, etc. Cinemas offer specially reduced prices to troops—where are they close to each other is the City—No. 27 on Map.

NOON PAUSE. At 12 noon a two minutes' silence for wartime prayer is observed by Cape Town at noon daily. Remember to halt and remain at attention when you hear the noon gun.

NOTE that in South Africa bars and licensed premises are always closed on Sundays.

PLACES OF INTEREST.

TABLE MOUNTAIN AERIAL CABLEWAY. Enables visitors to reach the top of Table Mountain ; in operation every day, weather permitting, at a special fare of 5s. Take Tram No. 1 in St. George's Street to terminus at Kloof Nek, and Cableway bus thence (fare 6d.) to lower Cableway Station.

BOTANICAL GARDENS. In Avenue, leading from top of Adderley Street (No. 20 on Map).

MUSEUMS AND ART GALLERIES.
SOUTH AFRICAN MUSEUM, top of Avenue (No. 16 on Map) beyond Botanical Gardens.
KOOPMANS-DE WET MUSEUM, 35 Strand Street (No. 26 on Map). Collection of old colonial furniture and antiques.
SOUTH AFRICAN ART GALLERY, Avenue, opposite Museum (No. 15 on Map).
MICHAELIS ART GALLERY, Greenmarket Square (No. 24 on Map). Fine collection of Dutch paintings.
SOUTH AFRICAN LIBRARY.
Avenue (No. 15 on Map), at foot of Botanical Gardens. Free Reading Rooms, etc.

Compiled and Published by THE CAPE PENINSULA PUBLICITY ASSOCIATION VISITORS' INFORMATION BUREAU, CAPE TOWN

DON'T TALK ABOUT SHIPS OR SHIPPING!

MAP OF CENTRAL CAPE TOWN

You enter the City from the Docks at this point

INFORMATION KIOSK HERE

PRINCIPAL STREET OF CITY

TABLE BAY

TABLE MOUNTAIN LIES IN THIS DIRECTION

1 October 1942

My Own Darling

Well, your letters are beginning to arrive and are a great tonic, believe me. I haven't got quite the hang of how we stand yet as I have just received your birthday greetings which should I think have arrived before your last one. It arrived just a month after my birthday but much better late than never my dear. Please thank Marion for her nice card. I think she done it very well. I have sent her a long letter but I don't suppose she will get it until about Xmas time. Now I have just received your Air Mail and thank goodness in good time before black out. Your first three I did not get until later in the day and I did not get a chance to open them before it was dark so in my pocket they had to stay until morning. What torture!! Well, my darling I am glad you got home. It would make a nice change for you but you seem to be having a busy time now however so long as you are happy that's all that matters. I received an Air Mail from Brenda the same time as yours. I have not written to her yet as for one thing I was not sure where she would be and we are only allowed one of these Air Mails a week. However, when I can get some ink, I will send her an airgraph. They are not quite so convenient as these as they have to be written in ink and have to be kept flat so just imagine one's patience trying to get one ready with ten million flies around one's head and a dust storm brewing in the offing. I sent you two my dear so hope you were able to read them. I hope you found your Ma and Pa quite well. You didn't say much about what sort of a place they had and if you like it any better than the previous ones. I do hope you will be able to stay in the wee lodge for apart from the long winter months.

I do really think you are much better there than anywhere else at these trying times, and if I am lucky enough to be amongst the fortunate for some reason, I feel that is where I would like to return to. However, we will just have to wait and see and of course my darling wherever you and the children may be, safe and well, is all that will matter to me. I am greatly looking forward to the photo which Marion tells is coming. Of course, I have these others which I cherish and unfortunately, I find I cannot get my wallet in my K.D shirt pockets. I did carry just the photos themselves but I found they were getting spoilt with the heat, sweat etc so back they went into the wallet but it is very often brought out. If you have Harold's address will you send it next time. I find I haven't got it. If you haven't got it either it doesn't matter as I have Marjorie's so I will send one through her. I feel I should write to him. I am glad you got to the pictures. Did you go at Leyburn? I hope you will get the chance to see some nice pictures sometimes. I did see "Next of Kin" after all, on the boat. I thought the cinema in mid ocean was a great thrill. I saw two other films, "Alexander's Rag Time Band" and "Kidnapped". Both very good, the latter being mostly of Scotland. Was the first letter you received in the green envelope? I am wondering if you received that one. I wrote it an hour after getting aboard and it went before we sailed. The second one is the one you got at home I should think. After that I sent Marion a letter and you an airgraph from the sea so no doubt you have these by now. Well, my darling I must close now. Every day that goes by is one day nearer the end of the war. We seem to have Jerry where we want him here now so hope we keep him there. I have christened my truck with your name in silver (paper) on the radiator guard so hope it brings us luck!

Bye bye darling. All my love to you all. Ever yours
Harold
Xxxxxxx

Don't forget a few eats if you can manage them. You know the kind of biscuits I like! Cheerio. Keep smiling. I sent Broadfoot an Air Mail when I sent your last one.

Marion and Ann, April 1943

Marion and Ann bathing, and in school uniform, 1943

My Own Darling

Thank you very much for the P.O I have just received but you shouldn't do it really as I know there are probably several things you need yourself. I shall probably buy some eats and extra smokes when next we get the chance to send to a canteen, when that will be goodness knows, however when I do, I shall enjoy it and as you say I will think of it as a present from you. Yes, my darling you won't be any more pleased than I am when this is over but when goodness knows. It still seems to go on and on although we have made such a great advance and he certainly got a whacking but there seems no end to the blighter. I am certainly doing what you say but at times it is very difficult, however so far so good. I am feeling better than I did when last I wrote. My adenitis has gone and I just have one leg sore left which seems a devil to get rid of. You say it was Sunday when you wrote your letter. This is a Monday I believe. We never seem to know what day it is out here. They are all alike. Sometimes I have had to ask half a dozen lads before finding out what day it is and, believe it or not, I have heard some red hot arguments as which day it was Sat, Sun or Monday. I am glad you have heard from my Aunt and hope she comes to see you. It would be nice for you to go to Southport too and I should if you get the chance later on, but I hope you won't get bombed. Oh, I heard from my cousin at Slough and he tells me he was married on Aug 23rd. Apparently, he is still living at home and she is still carrying on with the W.A.A.F.S. Well darling I hope you are getting all my mail. My last was thanking you for the very nice photo which I was very pleased to get. I think it is very nice of you all. If only Ann had the same smile as on the other photo.

Probably the man was not quite so funny as the Dumfries one. How they are growing. Look like being quite young ladies when next I see them. Marion should receive my surface letter soon. I also sent a surface letter to the Col. and I have written to McMath. I sent it to Cardoness so hope he receives it some time. The weather here is not so good, wet and very cold at night and early morning. Of course, this is the winter just beginning. I hope you are able to get some money to pay Craig's bill. Is that the old one? I hope you have not needed him since I left. Yes, my darling if you could just get a glimpse of me sometimes, I am sure you would not hesitate to keep your chin up. I quite realise how difficult it must be at times but you have done very well so keep it up my dear and keep smiling for nothing can be done now except carry on with the good work. Well, here's wishing you all a very happy Xmas in case you do not get another letter before then. Make the best of it darling and here's hoping I may be with you all for the next one.

Bye bye for now. With all my love to you all. Ever yours
Harold xxxxxx For those big girls xxxx

29 Jan 1943

My Darling

There are no air mail letter cards available so you will just have to be content with one of these. Your last one I received last Wednesday dated Dec 3rd but I fail to see how you could have received one from me dated Dec 9th!! Hope you haven't taken to drink. So glad you had a nice quiet New Year's Day but you did not mention what kind of a Xmas you had however I have written to Marion asking her to tell me all about it. Yes, my dear I can imagine how excited you would all be at home when listening to the news. It certainly has been a great achievement. 1,800 miles in exactly 3 months so not bad going. It was a good sight to see the Union Jack flying over Tripoli. We are at the moment camping in an orchard outside of the town. Unfortunately, it is the wrong time of the year for the fruit! I hope the people have come into the other lodge as it will feel very lonely with nobody being near. It's a blessing the light nights are drawing near once more. I should certainly keep the garden going if you can, bags of veg for who knows, I might be in time for the green peas yet. We hope!! Well, my darling it is a comfort to know you are all keeping well. I had a letter from Ma about a week ago. They were all well there so you have no need to worry. Well bye

bye for now my dear. Keep smiling for every day is a day nearer.

All my love to you all.
Ever yours
Harold
Xxxxxx

Desert wallet photo of Joan and Marion

ACTION

Having arrived in North Africa in August 1942 the 51st (Highland) Infantry Division experienced its first action at the Second Battle of El Alamein (23rd October – 11th November), sustaining some 2,000 casualties. The bombardment began on 23rd October. On 4th November 51st (H) Division broke through to the Rahman Track and the Axis forces began to retreat. The Battle of El Agheila took place in December 1942 between the Allied Forces of the 8th Army and the Axis forces of the German/Italian Panzer Army during the long Axis withdrawal from El Alamein to Tunis. Montgomery ordered a huge victory parade in Tripoli on 23rd January 1943. By May 1943 some 50,000 Axis soldiers surrendered, ending the North African Campaign.

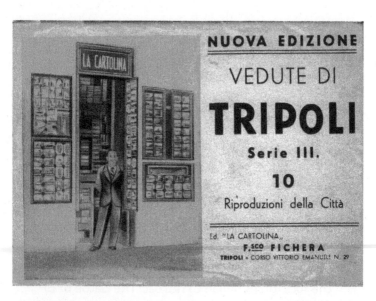

NUOVA EDIZIONE

VEDUTE DI

TRIPOLI

Serie III.

10

Riproduzioni della Città

Ed. "LA CARTOLINA"
F.^{sco} FICHERA
TRIPOLI - CORSO VITTORIO EMANUELE N. 29

Catania - Villa Bellini - Entrata e Vasca dei Cigni

My dear Marion and Ann

I have just received two of Mummy's airmail letters that I had begun to think had gone astray, one of November and one of December, telling me about Xmas which I so much wanted to know about. As I have just sent Mummy a letter, I thought it would be nice to write to you and Ann, so you can thank Mummy for them for me. I was glad to hear you had such a nice time at Xmas and I think you were very lucky to go to a big party again. I did not think there would be one with almost everything being rationed and so expensive, and then to another one at school, my word you were both very lucky. The book you had given to you certainly does sound very interesting. You look like being an expert in botany before very long. I expect you have really been a little disappointed not having had any snow for that means you would not have any snowmen to make and no tobogganing but Mummy tells me you have been sliding on the ice so maybe you enjoyed that just as well. Now I am wondering just how a bottle bomb managed to get on the shore. Maybe some military schemes had taken place there and it had got overlooked. Anyway, I am glad no one was near at the time it exploded and got hurt. I hope Mummy fulfilled her promise and took you to the pictures and I expect by the time you get this, it will have been such a long time ago, you will have forgotten! I haven't been to the pictures for a long time. It was to a funny little cinema when we first reached the desert. I don't suppose you ever thought there was such things as cinemas on the desert and 'talkie' ones at that. When we were in Tripoli I did not see a picture show but I did see two very good concerts. One was given by the Highland Division's own concert party and the other was given by the Kiwis (New Zealand soldiers).

This one had a very nice big band so there was lots of music. I was glad to hear you were being so helpful with the wood but I do hope you are very careful with that big axe. I really don't like the thought of you using it. You must be very careful if you do. How is the old garden doing? I remember you used to be a great help with the 'tatties' and I hope you keep the weeds down like you used to. Ann, I am sure, will give you a hand now. That will be the day when Daddy is back throwing the 'tatties' over to you again and a game of rummy before you go to bed. Let's hope that time is not so far away. I am longing to see you all again. I am glad to hear you are doing so well at school so keep it up and try and beat all the others. No doubt by the time you receive this Ann will have started too. Well, I hope she doesn't get the strap as much as you did when you first started. Well my dear, I must close once more. I hope you got my letter card in time for your birthday and that you had a very happy day and many more to come. With lots of love and big kisses to you and Ann. Ever your loving Daddy. Xxxxxx

18 March 1943

My Darling

You were asking me to send you an airgraph. Well, here it is. I will send the letter cards just the same but will send one of these in between. I have put the new address on here in case you have not received my letter card telling you about it. It is for air letters only. I was so glad to hear Ann was better. What a funny thing to get. I do hope it hasn't affected her eyes anyway. I have just received your air mail letter of Dec telling me about Xmas so I may yet receive some of the back numbers. I was disappointed Marion did not receive my birthday greetings. The one I sent Ma on the same day she received on 12th so can't think how Marion's could not arrive also. I have not heard from Brenda for some time. I suppose she is alright and still at the same place. Glad you got insurance premium receipt alright and I hope everything else is OK. Remember me to all at Cardoness and round about. Sorry to hear about Broadfoot and I hope Davie McMath is back and going on alright. Well Darling another day nearer so take care of yourself and keep smiling.

All my love to you all and I hope now you are all quite well.
Ever yours
Harold
xx xx xx

26 March 1943

My Darling

I am sending this airgraph to let you know I am safe and well to date. Thank you for your airletters and airgraph but what a lot of my letters must have gone astray for I have been asking for you a hundred and one things but never get enlightened however darling it is nice to be getting the up to date mail just now your last one being March 7th so keep it up. Now I can't make head nor tail of this parcel business, here's me been looking with longing eyes every day for the last two months as I understood you to say you had sent it last December but by your letter of yesterday it sounds as though you have not posted it yet! If by the time you receive this you have not sent it, I think it would be better for a while at any rate not to do so, as by that time we might know something of what's going to happen. I hope at any rate Jerry will have given in or jumped into the sea by that time. Well Darling I am glad to hear you are all keeping well and the children progressing so favourably. I am longing to see them and I pray it will not be so long as it looks it might be just now. I just received today a Xmas card from my cousin in Edinburgh. I note she posted it in November. Glad to hear Davie McMath is keeping well. Please remember me to him also the old keeper.

I will send you an airmail letter soon so bye bye for now
so keep smiling.
All my love.
Ever yours
Harold
Xxxxxx

1130250 Dvr Bishop.H.
243/61 A/TK Regt. R.A.
51st Highland Div.
8th Army
M.E.F

31.3.43

My Darling

I have today received another belated 1/3 (1 and 3) airmail letter of Jan 10th thank you for same. The mystery of the kitten now being solved. Thank Marion for her enclosed wee letter. I sent her an air letter card a week or so ago so hope she received it OK. I was glad to hear she had received her birthday one although it was late in arriving, however she would just have to kid herself on it was in time. Well darling I answered your last mail by airgraph as you seem to think they arrive quicker. Since then, we have been told not to put this full address on airgraphs so if you receive another with the short address on you will understand. I had another airgraph from Ma, hers seem to come through in record time taking only 12 days sometimes. She was saying there wasn't much room to write on them so I told her about the air letters for I don't think they could have heard of them at Leyburn. I have not heard from Doris for a long time so I hope she has not been ill. But of course, she usually sends 1/3 air letters and they take at

141

least two months. Brenda, I have not heard from for ages but of course she will no doubt be otherwise engaged. Harold is another person I expected a line from but so far not a sausage, so the majority of my mail is from you and after all that's all that matters so write as often as you can my dear. Gough has a fancy address sounds a bit base wallerish. My chances of seeing him are rather remote, but one never knows we might both be in Tunis at the same time. Anyway, the sooner we get there the better. I shall like it. If only it would finish the whole thing it would be much better still.

You would no doubt be relieved when you heard the news of our getting over that nasty obstacle the Mareth Line. By the way darling I hope you managed to get an H.T battery and were able to fix it. If I remember rightly, I believe I tabbed all the leads for you before I left. Glad to hear you are able to get to some form of amusement, it will help the long days a lot. I expect now you will be busy in the garden. I should like to see the rock garden flourishing when I return and tell Marion and Ann, I shall not expect to see a weed anywhere when I come home. It is very good of Mrs Ramsey to send such a lot of things from America and as you say is a great help these hard times. I hope I receive her letter you said you were sending on for me to see, for if I knew her address, I might drop her a line. Yes, my dear it certainly sounds as if the cost of living has reached its limit at home but you can just imagine what it is like out here, being ten times worse. The daffodils must be very early this year as you say they were all out a month ago, it must have been milder weather. It is getting quite hot here again but still keeps cold at night and early morning. Well darling I should like to think by the time you get this the church bells will be ringing once again, but I suppose we must just wait and see. I can't see how the blighter can hold out so very much longer, however keep smiling and hoping for the best.

All my love to you all and big kisses.
Ever yours
Harold
Xxxxxx

Picnic at Laundry Bay, 30 May 1943
(Marion bottom right, Ann bottom left)

Harold's entry in Marion's autograph book

THE END OF THE WAR IN NORTH AFRICA

The Battle of the Mareth Line began on the night of the 16/17th March when 51st (H)Division took the outpost line against negligible opposition. The main attack followed on the 20/21st March with another massive night barrage. The Axis defence collapsed on the 28th March and the following day 51st (H) Division was on its way to Gabes. This was the Eighth Army's last major set piece battle in North Africa and saw Montgomery force the Germans and Italians to retreat from their last significant defensive position in southern Tunisia. The war in North Africa ended on 13th May 1943 with the surrender of almost 250,000 Axis soldiers as prisoners of war.

In July the 51st (H)Division took part in the Allied invasion of Sicily which lasted for 38 days. Towards the end of the campaign in early August the division was withdrawn from combat and held in reserve for the Allied invasion of Italy. The division was then recalled from the Eighth Army and returned to the United Kingdom to prepare for the opening of Second Front in June 1944.

Souvenir photographs from Alger

1130250 Dvr Bishop H
243/61 A/Tk Regt R.A.
B.N.A.F

8 July 1943

My Darling

I have received your two air letters of the 14th and 25th so guess that is pretty well up to date. Sorry to hear you have been having such rotten weather for after a very lonely and dreary winter you deserve a little sunshine to brighten you up. I wish I could send you a parcel of it from here. It is simply terrific just now and it is beginning to tell its tale with me as I get very bad heads and my hands are covered in some sort of rash so I am attending the hospital and see nothing apart from sand and feeling hellish fed up. I am O.K. however I expect I shall be fit enough for the next show which is not very far away now. Well, my dear having divulged my state of health as you wished me to do so we must turn to yours. I was sorry to hear you had such a bad cold also about your teeth. It certainly was annoying to find the dentist not coming after making the effort to get that far and I certainly agree you would be better with them out so try and manage it before the cold weather sets in again. You know darling you will also have to see about some false ones as you will be a good many short and it will not be good for your tummy not being able to masticate your food properly, so do think and take care of yourself. It is a blessing the children keep so well and I do hope they continue to do so. I don't know quite what to say about Marion and her schooling. I am half inclined to think it would be better if she waited until her time was due to sit the control. I am very keen indeed that she should take every advantage of a chance of education. I would like her to learn languages especially French so I do hope she will be interested and want to learn. If only this rotten war would finish and let me get home to attend to my affairs.

However darling I know you will do your best to get things going the way we will wish them to go until that day comes and may it be soon. Sorry to hear about the wireless dear. You will miss it so in the evening. Of course, it has had its day really but I wish it had kept O.K until I returned. It may be as you say just the switch. If you could unscrew the little net in the front and pull the switch right out you would probably find it had a bit of rust on then if you gave it a little rub with a bit of emery paper you would find it would be O.K. Also, you must watch the leads of the batteries for they get corroded, so they need scraping occasionally. I was not surprised to hear my people were not coming. I know they used to get on Mother's "pluck" (cooks joy) but I quite understand how you would feel when your mind was set on them coming and it would have been a break for you. Maybe by the time this reaches you, you will be almost on your way to Stourbridge. I hope everything goes alright what with the crowded trains and air raids. It will be a relief to hear you have landed back safely. Of course I think you will find you will not be able to fly here and there very easily as the means of travelling will be very limited and by all accounts your journey has to be really necessary. Anyway, I hope you manage to get in to see H and H. Tell Harold I was disappointed not hearing from him. I wonder if you will occupy the same room as we had before. Not very happy memories my sweetheart for we used to quarrel like blazes!! It was just marvellous all the same and after all we used to atone for it on the hills at Kinver. Well to get back on the home front, things will be quieter when the Shorts go. Is there anyone else in view? I think you took on rather a heavy job with those loose covers. I hope you did not feel any aftereffects. I don't suppose there was any shooting last season. Have you ever seen Col John since I left?

I don't suppose very many visitors do arrive now with transport being so very bad. Now my own darling I must close as it is time for me to soak my mitts in some foul stuff like Condy's fluid. Where I will be by the time you get this goodness knows, probably sampling spaghetti in Italy. Remember me to McMath the old keeper and everyone else. Keep smiling my dear and in the evening when our treasures are in the land of nod and your thoughts turn my way still keep smiling and think of my favourite song "When day is done". I do every night. Au revoir my darling. Take care of yourself. All my love to you all.

Ever yours
Harold
Xxxxxxxx

P.S Just putting this in envelope when I got a surprise. A letter from the Col which he wrote in February.

36 — BOUGIE.— Hôtel Transatlantique et vue d'ensemble.

96. Route de Bougie à Sétif — Gorges du Chabet

Collection Parfaite — A.

Souvenir photographs from Bougie

151

13 Nov 1943

My Darling

I expect you have received my air letter letting you know I am OK. Anyway, I hope so but I am longing for news of you and to know you are all alright. I have not had any more of your letters through since I left 97th Gen. and those I received there you wrote in August whilst you were at Bates. It is pretty damnable as some of your letters must be floating around somewhere. My only consolation is to think you are all alright or you would have tried to get in touch with me somehow. If only I had known I was going to be here all this time (3 weeks today) you may have got a letter through to me at this address. However, my sweetheart we cannot foresee these things so must just patiently wait but I am missing your letters terribly. I hope you explained the situation to Ma and Doris, for being on tenterhooks like this I just cannot bring myself to writing to anyone. Darling you will understand how I feel. I am feeling much better in myself and gaining my strength back again. The beastly malaria left me very weak and the flesh just dropped off me. Of course, it did not help matters by getting it on top of dysentery. The grub is nothing to write home about here and the weather piles on the agony. The rainy season has set in so we are up to our eyes in slush and mud which makes it very cold and miserable. Nevertheless, I am very thankful I am not up the line for I believe the fighting is taking place in a sea of mud. I expect you too are having the cold dreary days again but cheer up my darling. Let's hope the bright and happy days are not such a long way off. We have really a tremendous lot to be thankful for up to the moment so just pray that it continues for us to the end. I hope my little girls are keeping quite well and behaving themselves.

Give them a big hug and kiss for me. Darling how I long to hold you in my arms again, sweetheart I wish some miracle would happen. I love you all so very much. Now I must say bye bye once more. I will let you know directly anything fresh happens. Au revoir sweetheart. Ever yours Harold Xxxxxxxxxxxx

ITALY

The battle of the Bernhardt Line. The first attack towards the Bernhardt Line began on 31st October 1943. By 10th November the British attack was running out of steam. The second attack was to start with an Eighth Army offensive on the Adriatic Coast and began on the 20th November with an attack on the Sangro positions. The Sangro was in flood and the approaches were soft and muddy. The adverse weather conditions forced Montgomery to pause and restart on 27th November. By this point the British had penetrated into the Gustav line and the Germans were determined to hold on as long as possible. The resulting Battle of Ortona (by Canadian troops) led to an Allied victory but the cost was high and a harsh winter effectively brought the Eighth Army offensive to a halt.

The push towards Rome was resumed in spring 1944 and the final offensive in April 1945 saw the Eighth Army move rapidly northwards. The campaign ended when the Italian army surrendered unconditionally on 2nd May 1945. One week later, Germany tendered its formal Instrument of Surrender.

Serial No. *MT/1433* ...... Army Form A:2038

WAR DEPARTMENT DRIVING PERMIT

(Not valid for driving any mechanically propelled
vehicle for private purposes)

Issued under the conditions of A.C.I.699 of 1942.

The undersigned *D.I.C. BISHOP. H. 1130250*

(description) *HGT. 5'-7½" Eyes - Blue*

Com. - Fresh - Hair - Dark.

being employed on Military Service is hereby authorised by the Secretary of State for War to drive
mechanically propelled vehicles of:—

~~All~~ Groups
~~Group I~~
    ,, ~~III~~ } (Delete Groups
    ,, ~~IV.~~ inapplicable)
    ,, ~~VI~~

when on Government duty, from... *9TH AUG.* 1945

until... *31 Dec* 1945

H Bishop.   *F. Parminter*
Signature of Holder   Permanent Under-
W.S.C. 51-5439   Secretary of State for War.

8RD
R.A. RESERVE
"M.T."
REGIMENT
(FIELD)

R. Wood / Capt.

Officer I/c M.T.
3rd R.A. Reserve Regiment (Field)

155

HOME AGAIN

Harold's letters home end there. Following his period in the transit camp recovering from malaria and dysentery, Harold may not have been fit enough to return to front line service. He appears, however, to have been retained as a driver in the 3rd Royal Artillery Reserve Regiment until late 1945.

When he was demobbed at the end of the Second World War there was no need for a butler at Cardoness House anymore. Over the next five years the family lived in five different tied cottages while Harold worked as a gardener-handyman or chauffeur at big houses across England.

In 1950 Harold and Joan finally bought a house of their own in Cowley, Oxford where they remained until their respective deaths. Joan continued to work hard as a nurse and carer. Harold was employed as a security guard at the car factory in Cowley until his retirement.

RELEASE LEAVE CERTIFICATE

Army Form X 202/A

Army No. *1130250* Present Rank *GNR.*

Surname (Block Letters) *BISHOP*

Christian Name/s *HAROLD*

Unit, Regt. or Corps. *3rd* R.A. *Reserve* Regiment

3 NOV 1945

Date of: *Last enlistment

*Calling up for military service *11.9.41*
* Strike out whichever is inapplicable.

(a) Trade on enlistment *BUTLER*

(c) Service Trade —

(b) Trade courses and trade tests passed —

(d) Any other qualification for civilian employment —

Military Conduct: *Exemplary*

Testimonial: *a steady type. works well, and is a reliable worker. honest and trustworthy.*

Unit overseas or U.K. Stamp

3rd R.A. Reserve Regiment (Field)

Place *EXETER* Date *2 NOV 1945*

Officer's Signature

Signature of Soldier *H. Bishop*

* Army Education Record (including particulars under (a), (b), (c) and (d) below).
This Section will not be filled in until the receipt of further War Office Instructions.

(a) Type of course.	(b) Length.	(c) Total hours of Instruction.	(d) Record of achievement.
(i)*			
(ii)*			
(iii)*			
(iv)*			

* Instructors will insert the letter " I " here to indicate that in their case the record refers to courses in which they have acted as Instructors.

Signature of Unit Education Officer.

POSITION OF SOLDIER ON TERMINATION OF RELEASE LEAVE

1. A regular soldier with Reserve service to complete will be transferred to the Royal Army Reserve and will receive Reserve pay until his period of Reserve service has been completed. If on that date the Emergency still exists, he will cease to draw Reserve pay, and will then-be transferred to Army Reserve Class "Z" (unpaid).
2. A regular soldier who has completed his Colour and Reserve service engagement will be transferred to Army Reserve Class "Z" (unpaid).
3. All other soldiers will be transferred to Army Reserve Class "Z" or Class "Z" (T).
   SPECIAL NOTE.—Army Reservists are liable to recall to the colours, if necessary, during the continuing period of the Emergency.

Notes: (i) Further details of service and of medals to which entitled may be had on application to O i/c Records, accompanied by the applicant's A.B.64, Part I.
(ii) If this certificate is lost or mislaid, no duplicate can be obtained.
(iii) Any alterations of the particulars given in this certificate may render the holder liable to prosecution under the Seamen's and Soldiers' False Characters Act, 1906.

THE ABOVE-NAMED MAN PROCEEDED ON RELEASE LEAVE ON THE DATE SHOWN IN THE MILITARY DISPERSAL UNIT STAMP OPPOSITE.

N.B.—A certificate showing the date of transfer to the appropriate Army Reserve (A.F. X 202/B) will be issued by the Officer i/c Record Office.

Military Dispersal Unit Stamp.

MILITARY DISPERSAL UNIT
No. 1
3 NOV 1945
EDINBURGH

WITNEY JOINT

5.98

FOOD OFFICE

APPENDIX

*Harold, his mother Marion, and his two aunts (left),
and father Charles Bishop (right)*

Joan's parents, Herbert and Margaret Roper

Joan's sister Brenda with ferrets ready for rabbiting

Harold aged 9 (marked x) at Fourth Avenue Boy's School

Young Harold, before his marriage (left)
Joan and Marion (right)

Joan on Harold's motorbike

Marion

Cardoness House, 2017

Angus Gillespie, family and friends on Drumore

The McCormacks outside their retirement cottage

Marion with Mrs Broadfoot

Marion

Marion

Marion, Ann and friends

Harold's relatives Elsie and Doris

Joan's sister Doris and Dick

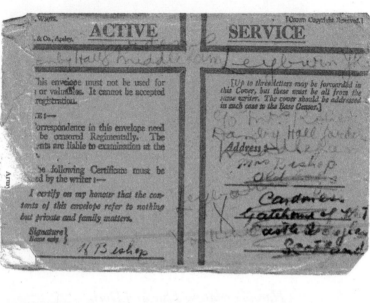

Ranby Hall Middleham ... Leyburn YK

To Mr Bishop
Ranby Hall Garden
Address:
Mrs Bishop
Old ...

Candmen
Gatehouse of Fleet
Castle Douglas
Scotland

51—1080

Opened
by
Censor

Harold and partner in the mixed doubles, 1930s (left)
Playing hockey (right)

A picnic on Cardoness shore, 1941
(Marion far left, Ann 3rd from left)

THE COMMANDER, OFFICERS
AND SHIP'S COMPANY WISH
YOU GOOD LUCK, GOD SPEED
AND A SAFE RETURN

Menu

Cream of Tomato

Fillet of Plaice Meuniere

Roast Stuffed Turkey
Buttered Green Beans
Boiled and Fondante Potatoes

COLD BUFFET
Roast Lamb   Ox Tongue
Salad

Apple Parisienne
Savoury --- Sardines on Toast
Fresh Fruit
Coffee

DINER
AU REVOIR

TUESDAY,
AUGUST 11, 1942.

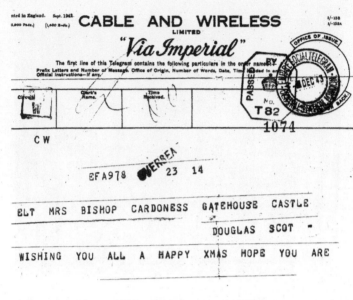

Chrismas telegram, 1943

*Italian cloth uniform insignia 'souvenirs': Tri-colour
Cockade of Italy and Horse Artillery (2nd Division)*

Cigarette case: the inside has been marked by Harold
with a record of his travels

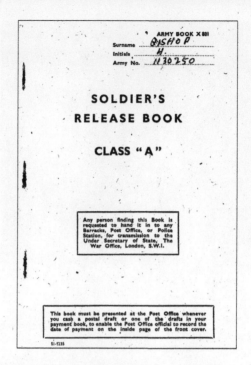

ARMY BOOK X 801

Surname ...... *BISHOP* ......

Initials ...... *H* ......

Army No. ...... *1130250* ......

SOLDIER'S
RELEASE BOOK

CLASS "A"

Any person finding this Book is requested to hand it in to any Barracks, Post Office, or Police Station, for transmission to the Under Secretary of State, The War Office, London, S.W.I.

This book must be presented at the Post Office whenever you cash a postal draft or one of the drafts in your payment book, to enable the Post Office official to record the date of payment on the inside page of the front cover.

51-5235

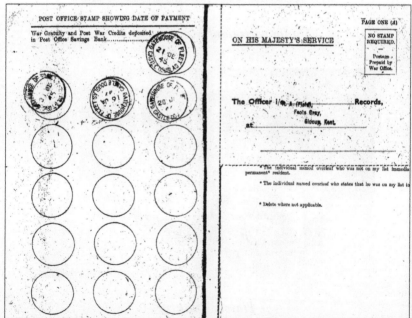

POST OFFICE STAMP SHOWING DATE OF PAYMENT

War Gratuity and Post War Credits deposited in Post Office Savings Bank ....

PAGE ONE (A)

ON HIS MAJESTY'S SERVICE

NO STAMP REQUIRED.

Postage Prepaid by War Office.

The Officer I/c ... *(Field)*, ... Records,

Foots Cray,

at .... Sidcup, Kent.

* The individual named overleaf who was not on my list immedia permanent* resident.

* The individual named overleaf who states that he was on my list in

* Delete where not applicable.

Studio portrait of Marion and Ann

Harold's first car

ACKNOWLEDGEMENTS

All photographs used in this book are reproduced by kind permission of Marion Gunther. Additional background information used for the introduction and epilogue was drawn from Flounders for Tea: Recollections of a Galloway childhood 1934-1945 by Marion Gunther (FastPrint Publishing, 2016).

Thank you to Annie Winner (editor of Flounders for Tea) for all the advice and useful information.

Thank you to Jacob Wise, Myra King and Lt Col (Retired) Robert Dixon OBE at the Soldiers of Gloucestershire Museum for helping me to identify the Italian cloth insignia.

Thank you to my brother, Mark Lothar Gunther, for keeping the cigarette case safe.

Thank you to my partner, Gareth McMillan, and my daughter, Rebecca Marion Croft, for their continued support and encouragement.

Thank you to my mother, Marion Gunther, for the many hours spent going through the family photograph albums, researching dates, names and places.

Thank you to Lorna Brookes, Crumps Barn Studio, for transforming my manuscript into this wee little book.